Your Best You provides a guided process of self-development as Bonnie Grove becomes the reader's personal coach. She uses her experiences of assisting others in making changes in their lives and provides personalized procedures for the individual who is engaged in change.

Pastors, teachers, and counselors will also find this book to be a very helpful resource. I recommend it highly.

—*Daniel R. Gales, PhD*, Retired District Superintendent
Canada West District, International Church of the Nazarene

Your Best You: Discovering and Developing the Strengths God Gave You provides easy-to-implement action steps to take readers from large, general goals to smaller, doable goals, utilizing creative solutions for making significant lifestyle changes. I highly recommend it.

—*Judy Rushfeldt*, award-winning author, speaker, and
online magazine publisher

The career I now enjoy comes as a direct result of living many of these principles. This book celebrates positive, God-centered change. It will upset, encourage, and inspire you to find your gifts and use them.

—*Phil Callaway*, speaker, and author of *Laughing Matters*

Bonnie Grove has written a powerful and practical guide for anyone wanting to build confidence, courage, and goal-setting skills so they can make the positive choices that will transform their lives.

—*Sue Augustine*, author of *Turn Your Dreams into Realities, When Your Past is Hurting Your Present*, and *With Wings, There Are No Barriers*

If you genuinely desire transformation, Bonnie Grove helps you unlock the treasures already inside yourself and shows you how to use them to make important changes that will empower you.

—*Donna Carter*, speaker, and author of *10 Smart Things Women Can Do to Build a Better Life*

Bonnie Grove offers an inspiring and helpful perspective to overcoming everyday concerns and living a more complete, fulfilling, and less worry-ridden life. Her Christian approach is grounded in years of careful self-observation and observation of those around her, and she displays a caring concern for the welfare of others. Grove's book is a source of practical suggestions and hope for individuals who want to examine their lives and improve themselves.

—*James Horley, PhD*, professor of psychology at University of Alberta
in Camrose, Alberta, Canada

Bonnie Grove cleverly demonstrates how we can optimize and use our God-given strengths in ways we never imagined. *Your Best You* is immensely helpful and practical. Best of all, it is life-changing!

—*Brad Burke, MD*, author of the series *An MD Examines*

Reading this book is like having a conversation with Bonnie Grove. It is high-energy, filled with quick, short sentences that make you pause and think—and sometimes laugh out loud. Along the way you discern that you have learned something good and helpful about yourself. She provides the motivation and the practical real-life methods for accomplishing goals. Most of all, it leaves you with a growing sense of hopefulness and optimism. A positive read.

—*Larry Dahl, PhD,* District Superintendant Canada West District, International Church of the Nazarene

Your Best You provides doable instruction on how to get unstuck and will help you develop momentum toward establishing the best course for your life. It's not just about getting rid of bad habits—although it is very helpful in that regard. It's also about discovering who you really are and how you can best use the particular gifts and traits God gave you. This is a down-to-earth, results-oriented, how-to guide to better living, to peace with yourself despite your circumstances.

—*Doug Koop,* Editorial Director, *Christian Week*

Bonnie Grove offers readers friendly advice, realistic examples, and practical exercises for making lifestyle changes. Whether the goal is to break a bad habit or strengthen a difficult relationship, Grove's book helps define goals and personal, God-given strengths. The author leads us through the process of breaking down goals into achievable steps and then applying a personal strength to each step. Using fill-in-the-blank charts, Grove makes it easier for readers to brainstorm about each step on the road to becoming who God has equipped us to be.

—*Bill Fledderus,* Senior Editor of *Faith Today,* The Evangelical Fellowship of Canada

Your Best You

Your Best You

Discovering and Developing the Strengths God Gave You

BONNIE GROVE

BEACON HILL PRESS
OF KANSAS CITY

ISBN 978-0-8341-2439-4

Printed in the
United States of America

Cover Design: Darlene Filley
Cover Photo: ® 2008 Jupiterimages Corporation
Interior Design: Sharon Page

Library of Congress Cataloging-in-Publication Data

Grove, Bonnie, 1967-
Your best you : discovering and developing the strengths God gave you / Bonnie Grove.
    p. cm.
ISBN 978-0-8341-2439-4 (pbk.)
1. Change (Psychology)—Religious aspects—Christianity. 2. Self-actualization (Psychology)
—Religious aspects—Christianity. I. Title.

BV4509.5.G6985 2009
248.4—dc22

                                                    2008055718

10 9 8 7 6 5 4 3 2 1

Contents

Introduction

Have you ever taken a good, hard look at your life and said, "Something has to change"? Have you ever tried to stare down a secret addiction, or, as they say, "just get over" your hurtful past? Have you ever been so scared of failing that you didn't have the courage to try to make a change in your life? Have you ever thought, *Everything changes, so why can't I?*

Your Best You is a book for those who have looked at their lives and thought, *I want to make a change, but I just don't know how.* This is not a one-size-fits-all approach to lifestyle change. This book is about *you*: how you work, what makes you tick, and how you can make the changes you need to make.

As you read, you'll discover your strengths and how your strengths can work for you. You'll learn to recognize your true goals and combine your strengths with those goals to create a map you can follow as you navigate the road toward change.

This will be a new way of looking at your life; you'll never see it in the same way again. The strength-based approach to change is unlike traditional approaches to problem solving. You won't spend time digging around in your past reliving unhappy experiences, and you won't put your problems under a microscope. You won't even be learning from your mistakes.

Why not? Because you've probably already tried those approaches. You don't need more practice looking at what's wrong. What you need now is hope. It's time to start looking at what's *right* in your life.

In *Your Best You* you'll spend time looking at the things you're good at—talents and skills; the things you love—people, places, hobbies, passions, joys; and the things that bring you joy. You'll learn how to build on your success by using your strengths. You'll explore all that's good within you—everything that's true, noble, right, pure, lovely, admirable, excellent, and praiseworthy (see Philippians 4:8). You'll learn to see yourself the way God sees you—a beloved child, His own creation, whom He filled with strengths, gifts, talents, and hope for the future (see Jeremiah 29:11). The Bible tells us that we are a wonder of creation. No other created thing was given the special attention humanity was given (see Genesis 2:7, 15-25). God has provided you with everything you need to succeed.

Be of good cheer. Do not think of today's failures, but of the success that may come tomorrow. You have set yourself a difficult task, but you will succeed if you persevere; and you will find a joy in overcoming obstacles (Helen Keller).

You can begin your wonderful journey of changing your life today. This is not a quick fix, and I'm not offering you a formula you can apply to your life to instantly become everything you hope to be. There are no special words you can recite, no one-minute prayer that guarantees success in thirty days. I'm not promising you a secret passage to a world where you'll be wrapped in a divine protective bubble where you will never again face problems. Instead, you're invited on a journey to a place of confidence and strength; a place where you have the assurance that God is with you, working in your life.

Change takes time, commitment, and faith. Pray now and ask God to supply these things as you seek His best for your life. God wants to give you His best (see Matthew 7:11). Ask Him. He won't disappoint you.

Chapter 1

What's Different About the Strength-based Approach?

A few years ago my husband, a pastor, and I attended a weekend of meetings for leaders within our church district. At the lunch break, the pastors' spouses were asked to sit together. Feeling bold, I introduced myself to a table of three other pastors' wives and joined them. As we ate, one of the ladies, a young newlywed, continually made comments about things she believed she wasn't good at. In a short time she had a long list. As we closed in on dessert, she said something that made my ears perk up: "I'm not good at remembering a lot of details, but I write things down. I'm good at being organized."

I smiled at her. "Good for you. I believe it's important to use our strengths. Improving on the things we're already good at is what really matters in life."

I heard a sharp snorting sound. It had come from another woman at the table. She punctuated her disbelief of my statement by muttering, "Yeah, right. Whatever."

I bit into a cookie. "What's the better alternative?"

She waved a hand. "People need to work on the things they're not good at. If there's weakness in your life, you need to work to turn it into a strength."

I finished off my cookie and reached for my coffee. "I don't think I'll be doing that. There are too many things I'm not good at."

The three women stared back at me.

I gestured to the room. "See all the people? Each person here has abilities, things he or she is good at—strengths, if you will. If I took all the strengths of all the people in this room and lined them up against the wall, there'd be hundreds of strengths I don't possess: things I'm not good at—things I'd need to work to improve. I could spend my entire life trying to get better at all of those things. And those are just the abilities and strengths in this room.

"If I spent my time focusing on the few things I'm good at and worked at getting even better at them—well, life would be much easier for me. I believe God gave me wonderful gifts He wants me to use."

The skeptical woman sipped her water and said, "But you said she shouldn't even worry about the things she isn't good at. I think the Bible tells us just the opposite."

I shook my head. "Actually, I said she was doing a great job using her strengths to manage something she wasn't good at. She's not good at remembering things, but she's good at writing things down. She doesn't have to worry about having a good memory."

This is the big advantage of the strength-based approach to making changes in your life. There is no expectation for you to fix everything you think is broken or improve your performance in areas you aren't very good at. It's time to stop overlooking your gifts, talents, abilities, and strengths. It's time to start putting them to even greater use in your life.

It's time to begin to see yourself for what you're good at rather than what you think you *should* be good at. It's time to begin seeing yourself for the miracle you are.

How Versus What

Have you ever seen a spiritual gifts inventory? They ask lots of questions about what you like to do and what things are important to you. At the end there is a formula to help you determine what your spiritual gifts are.

I took one several years ago and found that, according to that test, my spiritual gifts are mercy, wisdom, discernment, pastoral, and helps—in that order.

Cool! I thought. *What neat gifts!*

Then I asked myself, *What do I do with them?*

Well, that wasn't covered by the test result formula. I was told what my gifts were and given a brief description of each gift, but I wasn't told how my gifts worked and what I could do to use them. Just knowing what my gifts were didn't help me jump-start my personal ministry.

I was taught in psychology class that three important elements are necessary for a test to be considered reliable:

1. **Does it test for what it says it tests for?** In other words, does it measure what it's supposed to measure? If you take an IQ test, for instance, it's important that the test actually measures your IQ—not your shoe size.

2. **Is it a consistent measure?** If the test was given to two groups of 1,000 people each, would the results show a similar pattern in each group? In other words, is it reliable?

3. **What are the limitations of the test?** The limitations of the spiritual gifts test I took were troubling.

The test was limited to determining which of the seven spiritual gifts listed in Romans 12:6-8 I possessed. There was no way to measure any gifts I might have that were not on that list. It was good information, but learning the names of the gifts I possessed didn't change anything for me.

Over the years I've read stacks of research papers, magazine articles, and books about making life changes. I usually ended up thinking *Good advice. But how should I go about doing it?*

If there was any advice given it was usually along the lines of "Do what I do" or "This is what worked for me." I would read and think, *I can't do that. It just isn't me.* Sometimes I tried to follow the steps, but I usually grew weary of the effort and reverted to my old patterns, habits, and ways of thinking. I would become exasperated and exclaim, "It's too hard; I can't change!"

Then I discovered an important truth. It was as close as the skin I was in. The reason I couldn't find the answers in the pages of those books and articles was because I was asking the wrong questions. I kept asking, "What's wrong with me? How can I fix it?" I should have been asking "What's right with me, and how can I build on it?"

When I began asking the right questions, things began to change.

Dealing with Fear

When it comes to lifestyle changes, fear must be dealt with head-on. The most common fear I hear voiced is "I'm afraid I'll try and fail."

If you look closely at your fears, you will probably discover that they aren't as big and scary as you think. Imagine walking along a narrow mountain trail. You hug the mountain and take each step carefully, eyeing the outside edge of the trail. What is it you're so afraid of? Falling, of course! But you haven't fallen. You're on the path, moving along, making progress. Your fear of falling is based on the *possibility* of a future event. You're afraid you *might* fall. When we give in to fear, we give away our present joy and instead focus on an event that hasn't even happened——an event that may never happen.

The key to putting fear in its place is to focus your thoughts on the actual steps you're taking right now, in this moment. If you're walking a narrow mountain path, it's reasonable to maintain a healthy respect for the edge of the cliff, to be aware of it, and to walk in such a way as to avoid going over the edge. However, there's no need to fear it.

The same is true for making the change you want to make in your life. Yes, there are things you need to take into consideration——

things you must be aware of and will want to avoid if you are to succeed. But you don't have to be afraid.

There's another important reason not to give in to fear: God is
with you. He has given you the ability to accomplish what you need to accomplish, and His
desire is that you will live without fear (see
Romans 8:15). God created you with care,
and He wants to be active and involved
in every aspect of your life. You can see
how God is at work in your life—right this
moment. He has given you everything you
need to succeed; He's working with you as
you make a change.

Hope
begins in the dark,
the stubborn hope that if
you show up and try to do the
right thing, the dawn will come.
You wait and watch and work:
You don't give up (Anne
Lamott).

God.

Creator of all things.

King of heaven and earth.

Tell me, what is there to fear (see Romans 8:31)?

Self-generated Solutions

In therapeutic conversations, counselors often focus on helping
clients see important insights about themselves. These moments
of insight occur when persons come to understand themselves or
their situations in a new light or a new perspective. They're often
referred to as "aha" moments. These are the times when we get it
on a deeper level.

"Aha" moments are important. You've had them, haven't you?
Think about a time when you were in school or in some type of
learning situation. The instructor laid out concepts and ideas and
explained them, but it was up to you to make sense of all the components. You had to pull together all the bits of information and
make a complete picture out of them. When you did, that was an
"aha" moment. You were smiling, and you thought, *I get it!*

Someone showed the way, but it was your effort—your ability
to think it through—that brought you to that moment of insight.

That's where this journey is leading you. This book has resources, ideas, Bible references, and exercises for you to do. But there's another place, another expert source you'll be consulting: you.

You're on the journey of your life. This book is going to help you dig deep to find out exactly what is *in* you. You're the expert on your life, and, with some guidance, you're going to be able to find your solutions and make the change you want to make.

I Know Better

It's been said that knowledge is power. That's true—sort of. I spent one year researching the "process of change" in people and studying dozens of programs created to help people make important changes in their lives. I noticed that each program began by giving the participant (the person using the program to stop smoking, drinking, doing drugs, or whatever the addiction) a long list of information, facts, and statistics. It included good, accurate, up-to-date, and relevant information. For someone trying to make a change in his or her life, the amount of information was overwhelming. I was overwhelmed, and I wasn't even trying to overcome an addiction.

So when I began to design a program to help people overcome addiction, I asked myself, *What do people really need to know?* The surprising answer was—not much. For the most part, people already have the knowledge and information they need in order to make a change. They may not know specific medical details, like the effects of smoking on a developing fetus. They may not know academic details such as how support systems work in hierarchies, but they know a lot. They know they hurt. They know things aren't working well, and they know their addiction is hurting them.

Let's look at a pastor with a secret addiction to Internet pornography. What could someone tell him that he doesn't already know? He knows what the Bible says about sexual sin (1 Corinthians 6:18; Galatians 5:19). He knows he'll lose his job if anyone finds out. He knows it's affecting his marriage relationship in negative ways. He knows it's affecting his relationship with God in negative ways. He knows it's wrong. He knows he should stop. He could write a book about all he knows about this issue, but he still meets with his computer in the dead of night, gazing at images he knows are destroying the best parts of his life. What else does he really need to know?

Or take a young mother of three small children who smokes two packs of cigarettes a day. She knows smoking is bad for her. She knows it's bad for her children—harmful, even. She knows cigarettes have been linked to cancer. She knows her oldest has had a cold for six months that he just can't shake, but her life is stressful and she works so hard every day. Cigarettes are her only indulgence, her only consolation for all her hard work. She knows she should quit. What else does she really need to know?

There's a woman who can't stop eating. She's overweight, and she hates it, but she doesn't cut back on the amount she is eating. She thinks about her weight all the time. She's started to avoid public places where people stare at her. She's gone to different weight-loss groups, tried every diet book out there, but she can't stop eating. She knows she's at risk for all sorts of diseases because of her weight. She knows her blood pressure is climbing. She knows her knees ache all the time. She knows she's miserable. What else does she really need to know?

These people don't need to know more facts, statistics, or Bible verses. They need to know one thing: there's hope.

Knowledge and Empowerment

Knowledge is critical. The more we know, the more ability we have to reason out problems, make decisions, and think logically. However, research has shown that knowledge by itself isn't enough to change us. As I researched, I started looking into the nature of knowledge. I knew the Book of Proverbs is a book in the Old Testament dedicated to the subjects of wisdom and knowledge, so I started there. As I read, it became clear to me that knowledge and wisdom are extremely important to people who want to live a life that's pleasing to God (see Proverbs 1:7). However, I discovered that the nature of knowledge is a lot like the nature of love; it must be pursued in order to be useful. You need to go looking for knowledge. Only the knowledge you seek on your own brings change. Why? Because the knowledge you go out and look for is the knowledge you are most likely going to apply to your life. It's relevant to you. That's why you're looking for it.

The traditional approach to lifestyle change has, in my opinion, missed the first few steps needed to make a real, lifelong change. It usually jumps right to the information/knowledge/educational stuff. What we need to do is back up and begin, instead, with the person who is looking to make a change. You're about to learn how to find the knowledge you need, when you need it, in order to apply it to your change. It's called empowerment.

How Empowerment Works

Empowerment isn't someone else telling you what to do and then you go out and do it. True empowerment is the desire and ability for you to seek knowledge and solutions for yourself. For example, let's say a drug house sets up in your neighborhood. Terrible things begin happening—frightening things. All you want is for these people to go away. You turn to the police. They set up surveillance, patrol the neighborhood, and make some arrests. They do everything they can, but they can't uproot the drug house from your neighborhood.

You decide something can be done. You don't know what, but you're willing to do just about anything to restore your neighborhood to the peaceful place it once was. You take a single step: you pick up the phone and talk to a neighbor. Then you speak to several other neighbors. Soon, a neighborhood council is formed. People begin to bring ideas, resources, and contacts to the group. A media campaign is launched. Assistance from City Hall is granted. People from the neighborhood take turns patrolling their streets and reporting suspicious activity to police. Everyone stands up to the drug dealers, making life so miserable for them that they abandon your neighborhood. And it all started with one person making a single phone call with the belief that something could be done.

Notice that it wasn't one person doing everything and making everything happen. It was one person deciding that something could be done, then looking for the solutions himself or herself— making it happen, finding answers.

This is the journey you're about to take, the journey of empowerment, where you'll find the ability to go after the answers to your questions. Quite honestly, when you begin your journey through this book, you may not be able to clearly see how finding your strengths will help you make a lifestyle change. As in the story you just read, when you picked up the phone to talk to the neighbor, you didn't have all the answers, and you didn't know where exactly it would lead—you just knew you needed to do something.

A woman I was working with was using my strength-based program to try to kick an addiction. She told me that when she first saw the materials I had asked her to work through, she thought, *How on earth is this going to help me?* However, she was faithful to the process, and within *two months* she had not only kicked her addiction but also had made many other changes to her life. On my last visit with her, she told me, "Finding and using my strengths has made all the difference in the world."

What she managed to do was nothing short of incredible. While I worked with her exclusively on the issue of her addiction, she had made huge changes to other aspects of her life. She interviewed for—and got—a job (something she previously believed she was not capable of doing). She lost weight. She began communicating with her husband in new, more positive ways. She changed her circle of friends from people who shared her former addiction to people who were not addicts.

She made these changes on her own. I didn't help her make them. I didn't even know about some of them! That's empowerment. I helped her get started, but, in the end, she took control of her life and made the changes that mattered to her.

How did she do it? She didn't become Superwoman. She discovered and explored her strengths and learned how to apply them to her addiction. In the process, she found her true self—the one God had created her to be. She tapped into everything God had given her, and began to use them in an intentional way. Change was no longer difficult for her. Using her strengths, she was able to make several lifestyle changes simultaneously.

That's what your strengths are for. Part of the reason God gave you the strengths you have is so that you can live a victorious life, a healthy life, a full life (see John 10:10).

Chapter 2

Understanding Strengths

I have a mental picture—more like a video clip—of what it looks like when God decides what strengths to give someone. Perhaps God gazes down at a child (let's say the child is you), a big grin on His face. His eyes twinkle at the sight of you. An angel stands behind Him, holding an enormous book filled with every good thing—page after page of strengths, talents, and breathtaking abilities. These qualities are found in the Creator of this child.

The angel thumbs through the book. "Most Holy One, which of these gifts will You give this child?"

God's eyes dance with delight as He ponders the wonders He can bestow upon you. He doesn't want to rush this moment of joyous contemplation. He peers down at you, His smile growing. Suddenly, God throws back His head and laughs with pure joy. The sound is like every bird on earth singing all at once. Oh, He knows you so well. He knows what will bring you joy. The angel laughs with God. "Will You give this child courage? A love of nature? A sense of humor? Creativity?"

The Lord of heaven and earth touches your cheek. "To this child I've already given the greatest gift of all. I've given my Son so we can forever be connected in relationship."

Then God, overflowing with happiness, throws His arms over His head and exclaims, "But even still, I have every good gift to give. I'm generous beyond all human measure. The joy it brings me is uncontainable."

The Almighty God, Creator of heaven and earth, bends down and whispers in your ear, "Here, my child. These are for you. I give you these gifts. Grow in them. Explore them. Use them to bring glory to my name. Let them be a constant reminder of my great love for you."

Whether or not you're a Christian, you've probably read or heard about how God created human beings in His image (see Genesis 1-2). It's such an exciting concept that God wanted to be sure we really understood. He talks about it twice in Genesis. In the first chapter God, through the author of the Book of Genesis, tells us that all of humanity (male and female) was created in His own image.

By perseverance the snail reached the ark (Charles Haddon Spurgeon).

Two important points come out of these chapters that relate to you and your life. First, it's important to understand that *you* were created in God's own image. Yes, lots of things have gone wrong since the time of creation. Humanity fell into sin, and we lost the glorious connection we once had to God (see Genesis 2). The fact remains that you were created in His image, and remnants of His image can be found in you. Now you're going to look for them.

The second important thing to understand about the creation story is that God is active in your life today. You see, God didn't just slap you together and leave you alone to figure it all out by yourself. No! God has been involved in your life from the very moment you came into being. The Bible tells us that He was there with you, creating you, while you were inside your mother's womb (see Psalm 139:13). God wasn't just hanging out in there with you. He was busy shaping you, covering you with skin and flesh, and putting together all the parts that make up your body (see Job 10:8-18). From the moment of creation He has been with you, and to this day He is watching over you (see Job 10:12).

This is a picture of God being totally involved in every aspect of your being, your life, and your future. This isn't something you can hope God will do one day. God is already with you, working in you and molding you into the person you were created to be. He's with you right now, as you read these pages and contemplate making a change in your life. God is encouraging you, equipping you, empowering you, and leading you toward this change. Spend a few minutes in prayer right now, and talk to God about His presence with you as you begin your journey of change. Then write down some thoughts.

Take a moment to think about what it means to you to have God's presence as you begin to make a change in your life. Write down some thoughts about it:

_____

_____

_____

_____

_____

_____

Knowing God is working with you and for you as you begin to make a change in your life should bring you great peace. Yes, there's something you desire to change, and yes, it's going to take effort. But take heart, knowing that God is already at work in your life and is continuing the work He began when He created you in His image.

What does it mean to be a creation of God, made in His image? One thing it means is that if we go looking, we'll be able to identify something inside us, some quality that looks like God. In other words, when you look into yourself, there will be a piece of God looking back at you. God has given every person wonderful gifts. He gives them for a purpose. He wants you to recognize them as unique strengths from Him, and He wants you to explore them, use them, and enjoy them (see 1 Peter 4:10).

Let's begin taking your first steps toward changing your life. Answer the following questions:

1. **What do you love to do?** (It could be anything—a hobby, an activity, a behavior. For example, I love to daydream and pretend. Seriously. I love it. I asked a friend this question once, and she immediately answered, "Crocheting!" Don't censor yourself. Write what's in your heart. Remember: There are no wrong answers!)

_____

_____

_____

_____

2. **What are you good at?** (Things you're good at are often things you overlook because they're effortless for you. You can just "do them." For example, I'm good at remembering lots of little details about people I meet. I can run into someone years later and remember many details about our encounter years before. I don't have to try—it just happens.)

_____

_____

_____

_____

Your answers to these questions reveal, in part, what it means to be created in God's image. The things you love to do, that you're good at and find fulfillment in, are fragments of God's image in you. They are the treasures God has given you. These overlooked treasures hold the key to your success in life.

Look at your answers again. Is it an impressive list? At first glance, probably not. Mine doesn't look very amazing or astonishing, but they are things I enjoy. By answering these two questions, you've taken an important first step toward discovering your strengths. You've taken a first important step toward making the change you want to make. Keep going.

In the next chapter you'll spend time discovering your strengths. This is the doorway to answering the question "How can I change?" in a personal and authentic way. Stay with it, and you'll draw your personal road map to how to change your life. The road ahead is one of your own crafting.

Chapter 3
Finding Your Strengths

What are the reflections of God's image in you? Where do they live? How do they work?

It's time to change direction. From now on, you won't be just reading this book; you'll be working through it. It's an activity. It'll take thought, time, and effort, but it'll be worth every moment. Here are some things to keep in mind as you work through the rest of the book:

1. **Take your time.** Don't rush through the exercises. The more thought and time you put into your responses, the more useful they will be to you down the road. Remember—this is about self exploration; you're on a journey, not a sprint.

2. **Keep moving.** As important as it is not to rush through, it's equally important that you finish each section and continue to the next one in a timely way. At the beginning of each section you'll find a recommendation of how long each exercise should take you to complete. Sometimes it will be minutes, sometimes days, or, in the case of journals, weeks.

3. **Remember—it's a process.** While the exercises are laid out in a logical sequence, it may be necessary for you to revisit an exercise you've previously done or to work on more than one exercise at a time. Find out what works for you.

4. **You can't do this wrong.** I can't stress this enough. There's no way you can make mistakes. This is your unique journey. You're crafting your own map. If you spend some time going down a road that turns out to be a dead end, that's fine. It's never a waste of time or effort to learn something new about you. If you try something and find it isn't working for you, that's a *good* thing. You've learned something important about how you work. It may be helpful to write the words *I'm doing this right!* on a piece of paper and tape it near your work area, on the refrigerator, or some other place you'll see it often.

What Are Strengths?

Strengths are things you're good at. Sometimes we can identify our strengths in the things we enjoy doing. For example, some people enjoy doodling, painting pictures, making jewelry, or creating scrapbooks. Activities like these are considered creative and therefore would require the "strength of creativity." Other expressions of creativity could be writing, singing, acting, or other forms of performing arts. Also, our strengths can be connected to activities that don't include making something or performing. A person's creativity can be demonstrated through problem-solving, a perspective on life, approaches to new opportunities, or simple things like enjoying a good book.

Following is a series of questions designed to help you begin to identify your strengths. Before you begin, give thanks to God for every inspiration, talent, and ability you can think of. As you answer these questions, try not to think too much about how they fit into the big picture. For now, allow yourself the freedom to answer what's in your heart. Let your imagination drift; then jot down what comes to mind. It may be a word, an impression, a memory, a picture, or a combination of things. Remember: there are no wrong answers. Use the example provided to help you understand the process. These questions should be done in one sitting, in less than

30 minutes. You'll be able to revisit these questions at any time, adding to your answers as you learn more about your strengths.

Example: Read the questions first; then look at the sample answers that are designed to help you understand the process of answering. Remember: these are just examples. There's no right or wrong way to answer.

1. **Write down the things that inspire you.** Maybe it's a person, an idea, a goal, a book, a song, a poem, a place. Jot down anything or any combination of things that lift your spirits, give you wings, or fill you with hope. Examples of answers: <u>The character "Hadassah" in Francine River's *Mark of the Lion* books; she made me think harder about what Christian character looks like. Time to stare out the window on a rainy day. Upbeat music. Laughing. My husband laughing. When my children cuddle against me or sit on my lap. Seeing a friend after a long time and just picking up where we left off. A finished project. Not feeling rushed. My dog's loyalty.</u>

2. **What things do you love to do?** These are things you look forward to doing. When you get to do them, time passes quickly, and you feel absorbed in what you're doing. These things often take the form of hobbies or down-time activities—pure pleasure times. Don't overlook anything, even if it doesn't seem like an important activity. If you "get lost" in bubble baths, then write it down. It matters more than you know! Examples of answers: <u>Daydream. Read (especially short stories, non-fiction, and funny books). Laugh. Sing. Pretend I'm famous and people are asking me what I think about this or that. Chatting with friends about everything and nothing. Being listened to. Cooking and baking. Listening to music. Gardening. Organizing things (such as rooms, closets, drawers). Talking to myself.</u>

3. **What talents do you have?** Talents are often disguised as things that come easily to you. For example, some people can read three or four books in one week. You may think, *That's*

not a talent! That's just reading. But it *is* actually a talent. The strengths involved in being an avid reader could include creativity, critical thinking, love of learning, curiosity about the world, or imagination (to name a few). Examples of answers: <u>I have a good memory for people's names and faces. I think fast on my feet (most times). I tell good jokes. I'm always asking questions other people don't think to ask. I can sing pretty well. I'm good with dogs—I trained my dog easily. I take good pictures, especially pictures of children. I can look on the bright side of things quickly. I can whistle. I'm good at woodworking. I read lots. I sleep well every night.</u>

4. **What things do *other people* tell you you're good at?** Do you have a friend who is always telling you how much she likes your clothes? Do you often hear from people that you have great taste in music? Has someone mentioned that you take very good care of a pet? Do you get comments about how well you decorate your house? Do your friends and family turn to you with questions about math? Do people seek your advice about certain things? Do you often hear people tell you how friendly you are? Even criticisms can be comments about your strengths. I can talk a lot. This often isn't a problem, but some people find me too talkative, especially in a group setting. But it's a strength of mine, tied to my story-telling and creative abilities. It may rub some folks the wrong way, but it's still a strength. Think about comments from those around you regarding your strengths. Also, if you're comfortable doing so, ask a few family members, your spouse, or some trusted friends what they think some of your strengths are. Examples of answers: <u>Training my dog. My friends tell me they can't believe how well-behaved she is. Decorating my house. A friend called me "Martha" the other day! People say I'm friendly. My friend told me I have a good sense of humor. My kids said I'm good at playing with them. My spouse said I'm good at fixing things around the house. I've been told</u>

<u>I'm a good cook. My close friends tell me they trust me with their problems and secrets.</u>

Now it's your turn:

1. **Write down the things that inspire you.** Maybe it's a person, an idea, a goal, a book, a song, a poem, a place. Jot down anything or any combination of things that lift your spirits, give you wings, or fill you with hope.

_____

_____

_____

_____

_____

2. **What things do you love to do?** These are things you look forward to doing. When you get to do them time passes quickly, and you feel absorbed in what you're doing. These things often take the form of hobbies or down-time activities, pure pleasure times. Don't overlook anything, even if it doesn't seem like an important activity. If you "get lost" in bubble baths, then write it down. It matters more than you know!

_____

_____

_____

_____

_____

3. **What talents do you have?** Talents are often disguised as things that come easily to you. For example, some people can read three or four books in one week. You may think, _That's not a talent! That's just reading._ But it actually _is_ a talent. The talents involved in being an avid reader include creativity, critical thinking, love of learning, curiosity about the world, or imagination (to name a few).

_____

_____

_____

_____

4. What things do *other people* tell you you're good at? Do you have a friend who is always telling you how much she likes your clothes? Do you often hear from people that you have great taste in music? Has someone mentioned that you take very good care of a pet? Do you get comments about how well you decorate your house? Do your friends and family turn to you with questions about math? Do people seek your advice about certain things? Do you often hear people tell you how friendly you are? Even criticisms can be comments about your strengths. I can talk a lot. This often isn't a problem, but some people find me too talkative, especially in a group setting. But it's a strength of mine, tied to my storytelling and creative abilities. It may rub some folks the wrong way, but it's still a strength. Think about comments from those around you regarding your strengths. Also, if you're comfortable doing so, ask a few family members, your spouse, or some trusted friends what they think some of your strengths are.

_____

_____

_____

_____

_____

Identifying My Strengths

Now it's time to put a name to the strengths you've written about. Use the following chart to help organize what you've written. First, transfer your answers to the chart. Don't just copy your answers. Instead, look at each item you've written, and come up with one or two words that *sum up* your responses.

For example, in question 1 I wrote that I'm inspired by the character Hadassah in Francine River's *Mark of the Lion* books, because she made me think harder about what Christian character looks like. After I wrote that, I thought about what the character really meant to me; what was inspiring about her? I came up with an abbreviated version: Humble Christian walk. I put those words in the first box under the title "Inspire me."

Use your talent in every which way possible. Spend it lavishly, like a millionaire intent on going broke (Brenda Francis).

I also wrote that I'm inspired by time to stare out the window on a rainy day, and a bit farther down I wrote, "Not feeling rushed." For me, those things go together. I experience moments of inspiring peace when I'm able to take time out for myself. I put both of those things together and wrote, "Time alone to think" under the heading "Inspire me."

One more example of what I did to come up with my list: earlier I wrote, "my husband laughing," "when my children cuddle against me or sit on my lap," "seeing a friend after a long time and just picking up where we left off," and "my dog's loyalty." I looked at those answers and thought that mostly what inspires me about these things is the love I give and receive. So under "Inspire me" I condensed all those ideas into "Love for family and friends."

I did something similar under the column "Things I love." I re-read what I wrote and thought about what each thing means to me, how it plays out in my life, or what I like best about doing those activities. Then I summed up each of the ideas in a word or two.

This takes a bit of practice. It's pleasant and life-affirming to spend time thinking about the things and the people we love. Don't think that you shouldn't be proud or you have no right to think so highly of yourself. You're not being proud or vane. You're simply recognizing the different things you love to do and are good at. Then, you're acknowledging that these wonderful things are all gifts from God. It's not a negative thing to enjoy the gifts God has given you. In fact, your enjoyment is one of the reasons God gave you these gifts.

One effective way to deal with any feelings of guilt or upset that may come when you're trying to think of your strengths (things you're good at and enjoy) is to offer God a sincere "thank you" when you think of some lovely thing in your life. The Bible tells us that these good things all come from God (see James 1:17).

Use the examples below to help you understand how the process of filling out the chart works:

Inspire me	Things I love	Talents	Others say I'm good at
Humble Christian walk	Daydreaming	Memory for people	Dog training
Time alone to think	Reading	Fast thinking	Decorating my home
Love for family and friends	Laughing	Funny	Being funny
Music	Singing	Singing	Playing with kids
Laughing	Pretending/talking to myself	Training my dog	Cooking
Reading "good" books	Visiting/being heard	Taking pictures	Fixing things
	Gardening	Sunny personality	Being trustworthy
	Organizing things	Reading (lots!)	

Now it's time to begin filling out your chart. It may be helpful to use a pencil at first so you can add or subtract or change the wording as you go. Remember: don't write what you think should be there; write the truth about yourself with thankfulness to God for the wonderful things He has given you.

Refer to the examples above anytime you feel you need help. Also, refer back to your answers in chapter 2 to help you along. You may find answers there that were not repeated in the last four

questions you just answered. Add them to your answers, and be
sure to include them in your chart below.

Inspire me	Things I love	Talents	Others say I'm good at

Now that you've filled out your chart, it's time to look for common themes, repeated words, and patterns that will tell you about
your strengths. Below is the example chart from above. When I
read the chart by the column, I saw lots of different things that
didn't seem very connected. But, when I read the chart by the row,
I began to see common words, themes, and phrases that appear
under all four of the headings. I've highlighted the first example of
a pattern I found when I read the chart by the row:

Inspire me	Things I love	Talents	Others say I'm good at
Humble Christian walk	Daydreaming	Memory for people	Dog training
Time alone to think	Reading	Fast thinking	Decorating my home
Love for family and friends	Laughing	Funny	Being funny
Music	Singing	Singing	Playing with kids
Laughing	Pretending/talking to myself	Training dog	Cooking
Reading "good" books	Visiting/being heard	Taking pictures	Fixing things
	Gardening	Sunny personality	Being trustworthy
	Organizing things	Reading (lots!)	

Given that the themes of laughing, being funny, and humor show up under all four headings, I can safely say that humor is one of my strengths. I'll write "Humor" as my number-one strength. That's not to say it's my "strongest" strength; it's just the one I spotted first.

Another example of a pattern I found on my chart is under the columns "Inspire me" and "Things I love." Time alone to think, daydreaming, and pretending/talking to myself are similar. I know I love my quiet time, and it's only when I'm alone that I'm able to daydream and talk to myself. So these things are related. Together, they show up three times on my chart. That tells me they are important strengths to me. I've decided to call these things "Dreaming/Planning," because that's mostly what I'm doing when I daydream: planning out events, practicing for important conversations, and so on.

Inspire me	Things I love	Talents	Others say I'm good at
Humble Christian walk	Daydreaming	Memory for people	Dog training
Time alone to think	Reading	Fast thinking	Decorating my home
Love for family and friends	Laughing	Funny	Being funny
Music	Singing	Singing	Playing with kids
Laughing	Pretending/talking to myself	Training dog	Cooking
Reading "good" books	Visiting/being heard	Taking pictures	Fixing things
	Gardening	Sunny personality	Being trustworthy
	Organizing things	Reading (lots!)	

For my third strength I wrote "Creativity." Look at the sample chart, and pick out the entries that refer to my strength of being creative. These are music, reading, singing, photography, fast thinking, cooking, playing, and gardening.

For my fourth strength, I chose the words "Love for family and friends." To me this is a rich strength that informs every part of my life. I find I'm able to do difficult things because I have this strength and know how to call upon it when I need it. Look at the sample chart, and pick out the entries that refer to my strength of love for family and friends. (I actually wrote those exact words under "Inspire me." Under various other headings I have listed visiting/being heard, laughing, memory for people, dog training, and playing with kids.)

Last, I chose the term "critical thinking." Pick out the entries that represent critical thinking.

Examples of Strengths Based on the Example Answers

My Strengths: 1. __Humor_____

2. __Dreaming/Planning_____

3. __Creativity_____

4. __Love for family and friends____

5. __Critical thinking_____

Now it's your turn to fill out your list of strengths. Again, there are no right or wrong answers. Remember: it takes practice to think about strengths and then purposely use them in everyday life. In time, with practice, you'll begin to identify many of your strengths.

This list asks for five strengths for now. That's a good number to work with while you're practicing identifying and using them. If you find more than five strengths, then add them to the list. Make the list as long as you like!

If you weren't able to come up with a list of five strengths, that's okay too. You've done a wonderful job of starting the process of thinking of yourself and your life in a positive way. It may not happen for you overnight. Just stay with the process. Fill out the strengths you have discovered so far, and move on to chapter 4. As you travel on your journey, you'll discover new strengths. When you do, come back to this page and write them down on the list below.

Write down your strengths

My Strengths: 1. _____

2. _____

3. _____

4. _____

5. _____

Write out your list of strengths, and tape it up somewhere in your home or at work where you'll see it several times a day. It will serve as a happy reminder of the positive journey you're on.

Chapter 4

Beginning to Break the Addiction

Smoking, drinking, drug abuse, inappropriate sexual behavior (such as addictions to pornography or sexual promiscuity), gambling, overspending, and gossip are all examples of addictions and habits. The change you want to make may or may not fall into this category, but read the chapter fully before working on the exercise to decide if it will be helpful to you.

Getting Your Bearings

Have you ever gone hiking? One of the first things you do before you set off into the woods or up the mountain is to take a good look around and get your bearings. You look at the landscape and take note of any identifying features that will help you find your way back. It's an important step to take before setting off on an adventure, and it's important for you to do before setting off on your life-changing journey.

If you've decided that it's time for a change in your life, you may be tempted to jump right in and start making those changes. I understand that temptation, but if you're going to make a change that will last a lifetime, it's important to begin at the beginning. You need to look around at your current circumstances, how your life is now, and begin asking questions about what it is you truly wish to change.

Maybe you're thinking, *I already know what my addiction or habit is! I don't need to ask questions about it.* Yes, you know what it is, but you may not know as much about your addiction or habit as you need to know in order to get rid of it forever. In order to understand your addiction or habit, you first need to examine it over a period of time. You need to look it in the face.

That might sound unpleasant, but all it requires is for you to be able to look honestly at the thing you want to change in order to understand it. It might be a habit like overspending; it might be a pattern of behavior such as gossiping or losing your temper. Perhaps you're struggling with improper sexual thoughts or behaviors, or maybe it's drug or alcohol use. Over the next week or two, you'll spend time looking closely at the patterns and feelings attached to your addiction. That's all. You aren't going to try to change it. Your goal right now is to understand your habit or addiction.

First, when you're able to understand your addictions and habits, you remove a great deal of the power they have over you. Looking these things full in the face sounds frightening, but the truth is that once you do so, you'll begin to see their limits. They shrink. You'll begin to see how they can be overcome.

Another reason it's important to examine your addictions or habits is that you'll begin to see the role they play in your life—the purpose they're serving. Everything in your life serves a purpose. It does something. Even the things you don't like and want to change fill a need, satisfy a craving, or make you feel better. (Habits like smoking, drinking alcohol, and consuming drugs—while harmful—temporarily make a person feel better.) Understanding the role your habits or addictions play in your life will help you find new, healthy ways to have these needs met.

Last, understanding your addictions or habits will help you understand yourself, your routines, and your needs as well as your patterns of thinking and behaving. This self-understanding is priceless when it comes to making a change that will last a lifetime. You'll spend the next week or two examining your life as it is right now.

This exercise is ongoing. You'll work on it several times a day every day for a maximum of 14 days.

That's not as bad as it sounds. All you need to do is jot down some information each time you engage in your addiction or habit. It takes less than one minute to complete an entry. You may find you're able to gather enough information in one week. This is especially true if you want to change an addiction or habit or it's something you do several times a day, such as negative thinking, losing your temper, or saying hurtful things.

If the thing you want to change is not something that occurs every day (for example, I worked with a man who had a sexual addiction, but he didn't act out his addiction every day), it might take more than a week to gather enough information. Either way, spend the next week or two keeping an "understanding journal," in which you'll jot down details about the area of your life you want to change. Remember: you aren't thinking about making changes right now. You are simply getting the lay of the land. You are noticing the landmarks. You are being honest with yourself about what you are doing, when you are doing it, and how you really feel about it.

After you have the hang of using the "understanding journal" (give yourself up to two days of just working on it and nothing else), move on to chapter 5 *while you continue to fill in the* "understanding journal" *for up to two weeks.* It's important to keep moving forward in the process.

At the top right hand corner of the chart, you see the box marked "Behavior #." This is to indicate the number of times you repeat the behavior. For example, if you smoke cigarettes, you'll be writing down how many cigarettes you smoke as you smoke them. Your first cigarette is #1. In the next box you'll write the day and time. Then jot down a note about what you were doing and who, if anyone, was with you. Beside that box, you see a series of three boxes with faces. Put a check or an x in the box that best describes your emotional state *just before* you engaged in your addiction or habit.

Next, write down a number from one through five that best

describes your feeling of need for the substance or the habit. One means the need was low; five means you felt a high sense of need. Last, jot down a word or two that describes how you felt *immediately after* you used a substance or engaged in your habit.

When you make a mistake, don't look back at it long. Take the reason of the thing into your mind and then look forward. Mistakes are lessons of wisdom. The past cannot be changed. The future is yet in your power (Hugh White).

I've filled out two examples of the "understanding journal." The first example shows you how to use the chart if you're keeping track of a specific substance addiction (cigarettes, drugs, alcohol, and so on). The second example shows you how to use the chart if you're examining a habit such as inappropriate sexual thoughts (this could include acting out an inappropriate sexual behavior), gambling, gossip, or uncontrolled anger—to name a few.

"Understanding Journal" Example 1:

How to use this chart in order to examine and track a substance addiction: The example shows how a person who is addicted to cigarettes could fill out the chart.

Behavior #	Date/ Time	Doing what? With whom?	☺	☺	☹	Need 1 (low) to 5 (high)	How I felt after
1	Mon/ 7:30 am	Just woke up, coffee		X		4	Better
2	Mon/ 9:00 am	On the phone with friend	X			2	Didn't notice any difference
3	Mon 11:15	Coffee break. With two coworkers outside		X		1	Cold (chilly outside today) worried about the smell when I came back inside
4	Mon 1:30	After lunch. Alone	X			4	The cigs after I eat are my favorite ones

"Understanding Journal" Example 2:

How to use this chart if you're examining a habit such as gambling, sexual thoughts/behaviors/gossip or uncontrolled anger, and so on. The example shows how a person who is examining a habit of gossip/negative thoughts about others could fill out the chart.

Behavior #	Date/ Time	Doing what? With whom?	☺	☺	☹	Need 1 (low) to 5 (high)	How I felt after
1	Sun 10:30	In church. Talking to a friend about the pastor	x			5	Guilty. I think the pastor's wife overheard me
2	Sun 11:00	In church. Listening to sermon. Noticed a woman sitting near me dressed in jean shorts and a halter top. I thought she looked cheap.		x		2	Fine. I'm thankful I have nice clothes to wear to church
3	Sun 1:30	Lunch with friends. We got to talking about different people in the church.	x			5	Good! I love lunch with friends!
4	Mon 9:15	At work. Meeting with boss and coworkers. Got to talking about other people in the office.		x		4	Angry. I get so upset with all the office politics!

Understanding Journal

You may find it helpful to keep this chart with you as you go through your day. It's easier to jot down the details at the time rather than try to recall them after the fact.

Behavior #	Date/ Time	Doing what? With whom?	☺	☺	☹	Need 1 (low) to 5 (high)	How I felt after

Behavior #	Date/ Time	Doing what? With whom?	☺	😐	☹	Need 1 (low) to 5 (high)	How I felt after

Behavior #	Date/ Time	Doing what? With whom?	☺	☺	☹	Need 1 (low) to 5 (high)	How I felt after

Behavior #	Date/ Time	Doing what? With whom?	☺	☺	☹	Need 1 (low) to 5 (high)	How I felt after

After you've worked with your "understanding journal" for one or two weeks (or until you have enough entries on the chart), use it to answer the following questions. This can be filled out in one sitting and could take an hour to complete. You may decide to complete it in two sittings: one by yourself and the second with a trusted friend or family member who can help you see the patterns in your journal.

The example has been filled out by someone who is examining an addiction to alcohol:

Identifying Your Hot Spots

1. What time of day do you seem to engage in your addiction, habit? This is your time of day "hot spot" (circle one).

Morning   Afternoon   Evening

2. Where were you when you engaged in your addiction or habit the most often? (at home, at the office, out with friends, in the bedroom, and so on.) This is your place "hot spot." I often drink in the basement—away from my family. I also drink when I am out with friends in the evenings.

3. What were you doing when you engaged in your addiction or habit most often? (working, watching TV, surfing the Internet, and so on.) This is your activity "hot spot" I'm sneaking drinks from a bottle I keep hidden from my children. I keep one in the basement near the TV since I'm often watching TV or reading down there.

4. What was going on around you when you engaged in your addiction or habit most often? (alone and quiet, lots of activity, lots of people around you, and so on.) This is your environment "hot spot." I'm hiding mostly. I'm alone for the most part except when I go out with two friends who drink. Then I drink with them.

5. Look for spots in your journal where there are long gaps of time when you didn't engage in your addiction or habit. What did you do while not engaging in your addiction or habit for those long periods of time? For example, if you're examining your cigarette addiction and you see that you didn't have a cigarette between 5:00 P.M. and 8:00 P.M. on a certain day, write down what things you were doing that allowed you to go without

a cigarette for those three hours. These are your success "hot spots." <u>We went away for a week on vacation, and I didn't drink for several days in a row on that trip. I was with my children and husband, so part of it was lack of opportunity. One evening we had friends over and I didn't drink at all (not even a quick nip from my hidden bottle) that evening. It was a fun evening.</u>

Identifying Your Hot Spots

1. What time of day do you seem to engage in your addiction or habit? This is your time of day "hot spot" (circle one).

Morning   Afternoon   Evening

2. Where were you when you engaged in your addiction or habit the most often? (at home, at the office, out with friends, in the bedroom, and so on.) This is your place "hot spot."

_____

_____

_____

_____

_____

_____

3. What were you doing when you engaged in your addiction or habit most often? (Working, watching TV, surfing the Internet, and so on.) This is your activity "hot spot."

_____

_____

_____

_____

_____

_____

_____

4. What was going on around you when you engaged in your addiction or habit most often? (alone and quiet, lots of activity, lots of people around you, and so on.) This is your environment "hot spot."

_____

_____

_____

_____

_____

5. Look for spots in your journal where there are long gaps of time when you didn't engage in your addiction or habit. What did you do while not engaging in your addiction or habit for those long periods of time? For example, if you're examining your cigarette addiction and you see that you didn't have a cigarette between 5:00 P.M. and 8:00 P.M. on a certain day, write down what things were you doing that allowed you to go without a cigarette for those three hours. These are your success "hot spots."

_____

_____

_____

_____

_____

Your "hot spots" are places and times when you've noticed the most activity involving your addiction or habit. They're also places where you've noticed successes in overcoming your addiction or habit, even if they're for relatively short periods of time.

Now you're going to apply your strengths to your hot spots. This means you'll examine the places and times where you experience the most activity involving your addiction or habit, and you'll apply your strengths to making changes to your hot spots.

The first step is to remember your strengths. Even though you've already written a list of your strengths, write them again in the space below. Think about each one as you write it. If you've already discovered other strengths different from the ones you listed in chapter 3, write them down as well.

I've provided an example list of strengths that's different from the example list found in chapter 3 (to help show you the different things that could be considered strengths).

Example:

My Strengths: 1.   Spirituality

                     2.   Communications

                     3.   Organization/keeping a clean house

                     4.   Love for the outdoors

                     5.   Energy/enthusiasm

Next, you're going to apply your strengths to the "hot spots" in your life. You'll use your strengths to make changes to the different hot spots. You'll also look for ways you've already used your strengths in successful ways (look for your "success hot spots").

We are the hero of our own story (Mary McCarthy).

For example, if one of your strengths is your sense of optimism, find ways to use your optimism to make positive changes to your hot spots. If the kitchen is your "place" hot spot, you could use the strength of optimism by leaving yourself notes around the kitchen that say, "Addictions give you wrinkles" or "Have a carrot instead!"

In order to fill out the "Pulling Patterns from the 'Understanding Journal,'" you'll need your filled-in "understanding journal," your completed "Identifying Your Hot Spots" exercise, and some time alone. Fill out as much as you can in one sitting, taking about an hour or so. If you need to leave it and come back to complete it do so within one day.

I've provided you with an example chart of "Pulling Patterns from the 'Understanding Journal'" using the strengths listed above. You'll use your strengths list to fill out your chart.

To begin, fill out the column marked "Hot spot." You'll find your hot spots on your "Identifying Your Hot Spots" answers. Next, list a strength (or combination of strengths) you can use to apply to each hot spot. Then write down the different ways that you may have already used your strengths to make changes in your hot spots, if any. Next, list two specific ways you can use your strengths to make a change to your hot spot.

Use the example below to help you understand how to fill out this chart.

Pulling Patterns from the "Understanding Journal"

	Hot Spot	Strength I can apply to my hot spot	How I already have used my strengths to change my hot spots	How I can use my strengths to change my hot spots	How I can use my strengths to change my hot spots
My time of day hot spot:	Evening	Spirituality	I put several Christian books by the sofa to read.	I could invite my husband or children down with me to talk or watch TV.	Have a list of positive affirmations and scripture by the sofa to read when I feel like drinking.
My place hot spot:	Basement	Organization/ keeping a clean house	I keep the basement neat and clean and pleasant to be in.	I could have a pitcher of water in the basement and sip from that when I feel the need for a drink.	Add books about overcoming habits to the bookcase downstairs. I can read them when I'm tempted.

My activity hot spot:	Watching TV and out with friends	Communication/talking with others/listening to others	Call a non-drinking friend.	Go online and join a group that interests me.	Include my family in my evenings—maybe a games night.
My environment hot Spot:	Alone	Love for the outdoors	Go for walks with a friend or with my husband on nice evenings.	Do yard work, or chat with neighbors over the fence instead of watching TV.	Go with the kids when they walk the dog.
My success hot spot:	On vacation When non-drinking friends visit	Energy/enthusiasm	We can plan fun evenings with non-drinking friends.	I can get off the couch and get out more.	Plan an outdoor getaway for the family—to the park or a weekend at the lake.

Now it's your turn.

Pulling Patterns From the Understanding Journal

	Hot spot	Strength I can apply to my hot spot	How I already have used my strengths to change my hot spots	How I can use my strengths to change my hot spots	How I can use my strengths to change my hot spots
My time of day hot spot:					
My place hot spot:					
My activity hot spot:					
My environment hot spot:					
My success hot spot:					

The work you've done exploring your addiction or habit is going to help you as you walk forward, map your journey to freedom, and leave the addiction or habit behind forever. You've been honest with yourself, and you've explored the power you have over your addiction or habit simply by looking at it, exploring it, and writing down the truth about it. This is an amazing step. It's a brave step.

If you think you could benefit from more time examining your addiction or habit, continue to fill out the "understanding journal" as you move ahead in the book. It may be helpful to continue with the "understanding journal" for as long as you still engage in your addiction or habit. In time, you'll be able to swap the "understanding journal" for the "healthy living journal" found in a later chapter. You'll be refer-

Success is not a destination that you ever reach. Success is the quality of your journey (Jennifer James).

ring back to this chapter later in the journey as well. The information you've learned here will inform your actions in the chapters to come.

In the next chapter you'll spend time looking more closely at your strengths and becoming more intimate with them. You'll discover their full potential, and you'll be amazed at how often you've used them in the past to solve problems and work through difficult times.

Chapter 5

Giving Your Strengths Back to God

You have a wonderful list of strengths. What is the first thing you should do with it? Give it to God.

In chapter 3 we came to understand that all good gifts come from God. Before you began your list of strengths, you gave thanks to God for every inspiration, talent, and ability you could think of. Now it's time for the next step.

Look at your list of strengths. Read it carefully, thoughtfully (I hope this makes you smile). Each one is a gift from God, but for what purpose? Why did God give you those gifts? What does He want you to do with them?

You've already done the first things God wants: recognizing them as gifts and giving thanks. God has more in store for you. He gave those gifts to you so you would be able to accomplish anything you set your mind to (see Philippians 4:13)—like changing your life.

God is a personal God; He's been involved in your life from the very beginning. He didn't just stuff you full of good things, send you on your way, and hope it worked out for the best. No! He's with you now. He's actively involved in the journey you're on.

In the Hands of the Creator

In your hands, your strengths are amazing things. You can accomplish so much with them. But if you were to give those strengths *back to God,* and put them into His hands, then something beyond your wildest dreams happens. When you give your strengths back to God, you're allowing Him to work through you in ways you would have never been able to imagine on your own. Give your strengths back to God, and something better than amazing will happen in your life.

This is called surrender, and it can be a difficult step sometimes. I mean, you just discovered these wonderful strengths, and now I'm asking you to give them away. But the thing about God is, the more of yourself you give to Him, the more of himself He gives you in return. Jesus demonstrated God's desire to give back to us more than we give Him in John 6. Here Jesus takes a small boy's lunch and feeds 5,000 people with it, and 12 baskets of leftovers are collected—a snack for the long walk home, I suspect.

God has given you great strengths, and He wants to give you even more good things. Why? Because He loves you. Yes, it's that simple.

Love. Say it out loud: "God loves me."

So if God loves you, why does He want you to give your strengths to Him? Doesn't He want you to have them? Was He just kidding?

I went to a quilt sale once and found a stunning quilt. I fell in love with it. I stood admiring the handwork, the details, the stitching, the complex yet beautiful pattern. I pictured it on my bed. A woman who looked to be about 80 years old was watching me admire the quilt. She asked me what I thought of it, and I told her it was the most beautiful quilt I had ever seen. She picked up the edge and pointed to something. "Did you see the gingerbread?" I hadn't noticed that the border was comprised of thousands of tiny gingerbread men that then, in turn, formed a pattern that ran around the quilt. She pointed out more details about the quilt that my eyes had missed. Finally I looked at her and said, "You created this quilt, didn't you?" She smiled. Yes, she had.

I came away from that encounter with an understanding about God. You see, I had been able to appreciate the beauty of the quilt, but only the creator of it knew every secret, every treasure hidden within the larger picture.

And that's the way it is with our strengths. We can appreciate the scope, the wonder, the beauty of each of our strengths, and we can be thankful for them. But God, our Creator, is the One who knows every secret, every treasure within us. He can take our strengths and make them soar.

Listen now to the gentle whisper of hope (Charles D. Brodhead).

How do you give your strengths back to God? I don't believe there is a formula, but I think it starts with prayer. How and what you pray is really up to you. It depends on where you are in your life and in your relationship with God. It's personal between you and God.

Perhaps your prayer will be for God to show you what He would have you do with your strengths. Maybe you'll ask Him to help you notice when you're using a strength so you can better understand it. Maybe you'll shake your head and say, "I don't get it, Lord. Please help me understand." Perhaps you'll pray a prayer as simple as "Take my life, Lord."

This is personal. This is your personal surrender of everything in your life back to God. I can't tell you what to say or think or do. How you offer your strengths back to God will depend on who you are and what happens on your journey.

Have you heard the expression "Give your life to Christ"? When we hear this phrase in relation to someone becoming a Christian, it's said that the person has "given his[her] life to Christ." But becoming a Christian is only a first step toward giving your life to Christ. It's actually, an ongoing process. The more we learn and the longer we're in a relationship with God, the more we turn over our lives to Him.

The goal is to give all of us, our whole lives, to Him—the good stuff as well as the negative stuff.

Giving yourself to God means offering the best of us back to Him. It's an exercise of faith. It's a process, and at the end of the day we'll always find that God has given back to us more than we could ever give to Him.

Take five or ten minutes to write down a prayer, giving your strengths back to God. I've included an example of a prayer I pray, in case it might help you. Your prayer will be different.

My Prayer—Giving my strengths back to God: <u>God, thank you that I'm your child. Thank you for being a personal God who cares about every part of my life. No detail is too small; no problem is too big for you. Thank you for the wonder of living my life close to you. I give you my life, Lord, and all I have. Take it, I pray, and use it for your name's sake.</u>

Now it's your turn.

My Prayer—Giving my strengths back to God: _____

_____

_____

_____

_____

_____

_____

Further Exploring Your Strengths

In the next section you'll be spending time thinking about the details of the five strengths you wrote down in chapter 3. You should be able to finish this exercise in one sitting, taking, perhaps, an hour or two. I recommend you choose a quiet time when it's less likely you'll be interrupted.

Spend time focusing on the strengths God has given you. To do this, you'll write down a strength from your list. Then you'll reflect on and answer three questions for each strength. This is a pleasant and joyful exercise in which you allow yourself to see your life, your past, and your present in a positive way. You'll think about the times you accomplished important goals, felt good about yourself, overcame adversity, and met with success.

As you look at these important times of success and times when you used your strengths, you'll see how God was at work in your life during those times. Whenever you catch a glimpse of God at work in your life, jot it down on the line provided.

Use the following example to help you understand how to do the exercise:

My Strengths:

Strength #1: _Humor_

What does it mean to have this strength? It means I can laugh when things don't go the way I thought they would. I can see irony or something silly and enjoy it. It means I can be brought out of a bad mood with humor. I like to laugh and to make other people laugh.

What does having this strength look like? It looks like me goofing around with my kids, making funny noises, and saying funny words. It looks like me breaking the tension by saying something funny. It looks like me not taking everything so seriously all the time. It looks like my husband telling me he loves it when I smile.

How have you used this strength in the past? I use this often—daily, really. I use it to boost my mood if I need to. I use it to get to know people. When my son started kindergarten, I didn't know any of the other parents. I used humor to open conversations with other parents, and that led to new friendships. Once, when my family was going through a very difficult time, I spent time with my sister just laughing and saying silly things. It didn't change the situation, but it gave us both the strength we needed to keep going until the situation changed.

As you used this strength in the past, can you see a time when God was involved in it? I think God was there when I was laughing with my sister. It was such a difficult time, and we knew there was nothing we could do to fix it. We were relying on God to solve the family problem, and laughing was the break we needed.

Giving it back to God: God, I'm beginning to see how laughing and enjoying time with family and friends is a gift from you. It must be part of who you are to laugh and enjoy other people's company. Thank you for this gift. Let me use it to bring joy and not pain to others and to myself.

Strength #2: Daydreaming/Planning

What does it mean to have this strength? It means time alone is important to me. It means I have an active imagination—maybe a "childlike" imagination. It means I like to think things over before I act or make a decision. It also means that I like to prepare for social occasions (like parties or church functions) so that I'll say the right things to the right people. It helps me feel better about going to a social function. I guess in some ways it's like practicing to be me.

What does having this strength look like? It looks like me alone in the house, or maybe just in my bedroom—or the bathroom even. The children are settled in, and I have time to think about anything. I think about ideas I have, things I would like to do, people I would like to meet. Maybe I reflect on a conversation I had with someone. I pretend to talk to that person, saying exactly what I want to say exactly the way I want to say it. I get to be the "star" of my own daydreams, and things can go the way I want them to.

How have you used this strength in the past? I've used it after having a difficult conversation with my boss. I didn't like the way she was talking to me at work, so when I got home I went over the conversation again, this time saying the things I really wanted to say. It helped me feel better about what happened at work. It helped me when I talked to my boss later. I was able to say what I needed to say. I've used it to come up with ideas I want to write about. And I've even used daydreaming to decide what color I wanted to paint my walls; I just spent time daydreaming about what I wanted my house to look like.

As you used this strength in the past, can you see a time when God was involved in it? <u>I often talk to God during my daydreaming time. Prayer is a part of my "alone time."</u>

Giving it back to God: <u>Lord, I love my time alone to daydream and plan. Be with me in this time. Help me to keep my thoughts healthy and positive. Please speak to me when I pray, and help me listen.</u>

Strength #3: <u>Creativity</u>

What does it mean to have this strength? <u>It means I can come up with ideas at work that are different than those other people come up with. It means I like to think and create ideas—not things so much, as I'm not good at crafts, but I'm good at concepts, ideas, logic, and stuff like that. It means I can fall into a book and get totally lost in the story—which is a lot of fun! It means I can appreciate the effort other people put into things—like the school play my children were in or the concert at church.</u>

What does having this strength look like? <u>It looks like new ideas, lots of thinking, lots of sharing ideas with other people. It looks like me writing down my thoughts and ideas in my journal and then making them happen in some way. Also, I sing, and I enjoy acting and directing the plays we have at church.</u>

How have you used this strength in the past? <u>I've used my singing and acting to share ideas I have about life—and Jesus—with other people. I enjoy reading as much as I do because I'm creative. I've been able to complete difficult projects at work by being creative and coming up with ideas. Creativity helps me when I teach Sunday School or helps me explain something to my children.</u>

As you used this strength in the past, can you see a time when God was involved in it? <u>I believe God is behind my inspiration for writing projects and for acting and singing. I've often had the impression that He wanted to touch someone's life with my writing, singing, or acting.</u>

Giving it back to God: <u>You're the Creator of everything, and I believe this gift from you is so important. Take my ideas, Lord, and let them be something you're proud of.</u>

Strength # 4: <u>Love of family and friends.</u>
What does it mean to have this strength? <u>It means I have a place</u>
<u>where I'm always wanted—home. It means that I can have a bad</u>
<u>day and still find people who want to be around me. It means I'm</u>
<u>responsible to other people. It means I can do things I don't like to</u>
<u>do if it will help my family in some way.</u>
What does having this strength look like? <u>It looks like me giving up</u>
<u>a job to move with my husband so he can have his dream job. It looks</u>
<u>like me being able to tell my husband things that are important to me</u>
<u>and to be able to ask him for those things (like time alone or for him</u>
<u>to listen to me—things like that). It looks like me finding solutions to</u>
<u>keep my temper in check when my children try my patience. It's me</u>
<u>praying for my children—and for their lives and futures.</u>
How have you used this strength in the past? <u>I found a way to</u>
<u>work from home so I could stay at home with my young daughter. I</u>
<u>upgraded my education so I could be a role model for my children.</u>
<u>I talk to my husband often about my day and ask him about his day.</u>
<u>We plan family time. I've learned to be consistent in discipline for</u>
<u>my kids' sake. I invite my husband into the process of raising the</u>
<u>children.</u>
As you used this strength in the past, can you see a time when
God was involved in it? <u>I consider my children a gift from God—</u>
<u>my husband too. One of the reasons I fell in love with my husband</u>
<u>was that he loves me in a way that helps me be closer to God.</u>
Giving it back to God: <u>It's hard for me to "give" you my children.</u>
<u>But I know the love I have for them is from you, and you love them</u>
<u>even more than I do (that's hard to imagine!). Help me figure out</u>
<u>how to let go and to trust you more in this area.</u>

Strength #5: <u>Critical thinking</u>
What does it mean to have this strength? <u>It means problem-</u>
<u>solving. Thinking ahead. Planning. Organizing. Being able to see</u>
<u>things through from start to finish because I think it through first.</u>
<u>It means avoiding problems, or at least trying to see what sorts of</u>
<u>problems are likely to arise and trying to work around them before</u>

they happen. Looking at issues from many angles, seeing different points of view. Reasoning. Being logical.

What does having this strength look like? Sometimes it looks like daydreaming! Sometimes it looks like a discussion with others (family, coworkers, friends). It looks like me sitting down and wrestling a problem out by myself. It also looks like me multi-tasking, because for me, critical thinking is often doing several things at one time.

How have you used this strength in the past? I've used it to prepare for job interviews, in my daily job, in planning events at church or at home (concerts, plays, birthday parties) and in my writing (especially when I do self-editing of my work) Hey! I see a new strength here: I'm a *planner!*

As you used this strength in the past, can you see a time when God was involved in it? Hmm . . . sometimes after the fact, I look back and see so many holes in my plan or ideas and so many reasons it shouldn't have worked, but it *did.* Could that be God at work?

Giving it back to God: I believe you gave each one of us a brain to use. I'm thankful for the challenges I've been able to think through and the questions I've been able to answer in my life. Thank you for this amazing gift. Remind me always to check in with you, testing my thoughts against yours.

Now it's your turn to write down some of the details of your strengths. This will help you understand them better. Keep in mind—you can't do this wrong. This is your map you're drawing, your experiences you're recalling.

If you can't think of an answer to one of the questions, move on to the next one, then come back to the one you didn't fill out and try again. It may be that for one strength you find you have a lot to write about, while for another very little. That's okay. Don't force it. It'll come in time as you begin to work with your strengths in the next chapter.

At any time in the process you can come back to this section and fill out more details as you think of them. They can even be details about what you're currently experiencing as you work through this book. You make the rules and write down the things that are important to you.

My Strengths:

Strength #1: _____
What does it mean to have this strength?

_____

_____

_____

_____

_____

What does having this strength look like?

_____

_____

_____

_____

_____

How have you used this strength in the past?

_____

_____

_____

_____

_____

As you used this strength in the past, can you see a time when God was involved in it?

_____

_____

_____

_____

_____

Giving it back to God:

_____
_____
_____
_____
_____

Strength #2: _____
What does it mean to have this strength?

_____
_____
_____
_____
_____

What does having this strength look like?

_____
_____
_____
_____
_____

How have you used this strength in the past?

_____
_____
_____
_____

As you used this strength in the past, can you see a time when God was involved in it?

_____
_____

_____

_____

_____

Giving it back to God:

_____

_____

_____

_____

_____

Strength #3: _____

What does it mean to have this strength?

_____

_____

_____

_____

What does having this strength look like?

_____

_____

_____

_____

How have you used this strength in the past?

_____

_____

_____

_____

As you used this strength in the past, can you see a time when God was involved in it?

_____

_____

_____

_____

_____

Giving it back to God:

_____

_____

_____

_____

_____

Strength #4: _____
What does it mean to have this strength?

_____

_____

_____

_____

What does having this strength look like?

_____

_____

_____

_____

How have you used this strength in the past?

_____

_____

_____

_____

_____

As you used this strength in the past, can you see a time when
God was involved in it?

_____

_____

_____

_____

_____

Giving it back to God:

_____

_____

_____

_____

Strength #5: _____
What does it mean to have this strength?

_____

_____

_____

_____

What does having this strength look like?

_____

_____

_____

_____

How have you used this strength in the past?

_____

_____

_____

_____

_____

As you used this strength in the past, can you see a time when God was involved in it?

_____

_____

_____

_____

_____

Giving it back to God:

_____

_____

_____

_____

_____

You've made a wonderful beginning to changing your life for good. You've spent important time reflecting on the positive aspects of your life and giving thanks to God for His gifts and His presence in your life.

In the next chapter you're going to begin applying your strengths to choosing a goal that's right for you.

Chapter 6

Charting Your Course

"I know what's wrong. What I need to know is how to fix it!" my client cried in desperation. "I want to stop. But I can't. Every time I even think about stopping, I get so overwhelmed. It's just too hard."

This woman's words sum up how many people feel when they contemplate giving up a behavior such as an addiction to a substance like cigarettes, alcohol, or drugs. My client wanted to stop smoking marijuana, but it seemed too difficult, too big for her.

She had started smoking marijuana in order to fit in with her new boyfriend and his friends. By the time the relationship had ended, she was alone and seriously addicted to the drug. She was older now and pregnant with her first child. She wanted so many good things for this baby, but kicking her drug habit felt like a near impossibility.

That's when I introduced her to the concept of the "do-able" goal. I showed her how she could find out exactly what it is she wanted to change and how she could accomplish that change in small steps, using her strengths. She had the big goal of stopping her drug use, but that goal seemed distant, even unattainable. Why? It was just too big of a step.

Do you have a big goal? Are you looking to lose weight, break an addiction, change your negative thinking patterns, or gain control of your finances? All of these are examples of big goals. A big goal is the destination—the target. The way to get there is to take one step at a time.

You may be thinking, *Yeah, I've heard this before. I've even tried it, and it doesn't work. Even the little steps are too much.*

Be faithful in the small things because it is in them that your strength lies (Mother Teresa of Calcutta).

It's going to work this time, because I'm going to show you how to create do-able goals using your strengths. I'm not going to tell you what to do. I'm going to show you how you can know for yourself what to do. You're going to design your own solution using your inspirations, your talents, and the things you love—in other words, your strengths.

There's another reason this is going to work for you. If you've tried to change a behavior in the past, you'll recall the process was pretty much like this: identify what you want to change, collect resources regarding that change (for example, for a goal of losing weight a person might sign up for a weight-loss group, check out books about exercise from the library, or join a gym), then go and do the things you were told will get you to your goal.

This is a typical pattern for changing. It's what I did, years ago, when my big goal was to lose weight. It worked well. I lost 65 pounds and was working out five days a week. Sounds great? It was. Unfortunately, four years later I had gained the weight back and wasn't working out at all. So what happened to me? Did I change and then change back? No. I never changed in the first place. All I did was follow a strict set of behaviors for a period of time that got me to a certain number on a scale. Years later, as I was studying psychology, I began to understand the reasons I didn't keep the weight off. I discovered something so basic, so fundamental, that I was surprised I hadn't seen it before. I gained the weight back because I didn't really know what my goal was. I hadn't taken the time to figure out what I really wanted.

Maybe you're thinking *Isn't losing weight a good enough goal?* It might be for some people, but it wasn't for me. When I took time to think and reflect on my true desires, to daydream about the life I wanted and examine my strengths and the things I loved to do, I was able to find myself on my own map. (You'll be finding yourself on your own map in the next set of exercises.) I realized I needed a series of smaller goals first, before I could even formulate my true big goal. In time I discovered my true goal. My big goal, as it turned out, wasn't to lose weight. It was something else.

I'll share more details of my journey with you in chapter 7. For now, let's say that when I took the time to find myself on my own map and then applied my strengths to my journey, I found my true goal and was able to take my first steps toward it.

You Are Here

Life is a journey, and the first step to making a life-long change is to find yourself on your map. Think about the maps you see in the mall. You look for the "You Are Here" arrow that shows you where you are in relation to the entire mall. Then you look for the store you want to visit (your goal). Based on these two locations, you plot a course through the mall to get from "You Are Here" to the correct store.

Right now you're looking for that "You Are Here" arrow on the map of your life. You're looking for your location on the map. You're not looking for your goal (the store) right now. You're looking for yourself. You're getting the lay of the land and figuring out where you are in your life. The way to figure out where you are is through specific self-exploration.

Self-exploration should always help us "read our own map" in order to navigate the paths of change. Change is something that happens to us just by virtue of living on the planet. We can count on it in our lives. Everyone experiences change by virtue of aging. Life has stages, and we move through them—change—one at a time. However, deciding to make a deliberate change to our lifestyle is a choice we make. Knowing how you feel about making a change *at this time in your life* will help you navigate your way through your journey.

The self-exploration exercise is done in two parts. In the first part, you'll spend time daydreaming about your future. This is a pleasant and life-affirming activity. Take a few minutes to daydream about yourself, your family, and your dreams for the future. Answer the following questions as fully and honestly as you can. Remember: this is your unique journey. All answers are good answers.

It's helpful to write down the first thing that comes to mind, regardless of what form it comes in. If the first thing that comes into your mind is just a single word, write it down. Don't spend time explaining it or connecting it to a bigger picture. Just write it down, and then continue daydreaming. If the first thing that pops into your mind is a feeling or a sensation, describe it as best you can in as few words as possible, even if you aren't sure what to call it. For example, sometimes when I think of my future plans I feel a "whoosh" of excitement. If a picture appears in your mind, try to jot down the main components of that picture without getting bogged down in too many details. For example, perhaps you see a picture of yourself wearing sports clothes and walking at a brisk pace through a park on a sunny day. Write as briefly as possible the details—me, park, walking, smiling—then move on to the next thing that comes to mind.

Also, turn off the inner critic. Don't allow negative criticisms of your thoughts and dreams. Remind yourself that this is a time for thinking on the best parts of your life; the things that are true, honorable, right, pure, lovely, excellent, and worthy of praise (see Philippians 4:8). Dream, imagine, and drift into your hopes for the future. Hold hands with God and dream a little dream.

Again, there is no wrong way to answer. Any answer is a good one for you. You should be able to finish the following exercise in one sitting, taking no more than 30 minutes. I recommend that you choose a quiet time when it's less likely you'll be interrupted. I've included an example for you from the perspective of someone who wants to make a change regarding an addiction.

Example:

1. What are you looking forward to doing in the next year or two? I'm looking forward to doing some renovations on our house. We're planning to redo the kitchen and two bathrooms. I can't wait! I'm also looking forward to my youngest starting school next year. He's excited to be a "big boy" and go to school just like his older brother and sister. I'm hoping to have more time for my hobby of scrapbooking. I would also like to take an art class.

2. Write about your hopes and dreams for the future. Think about the next five years. What things will you be involved with? What interests will you be pursuing? I've thought about going back to school, maybe as an art major. I love to paint and draw, but I need to learn more about them. My husband and I are talking about taking a month and traveling around in our trailer, just to get out and see the country. I would like to be working part time outside the home—maybe in an art gallery or a theater. I want to get out some, but I want to be there for my children too. I would like to have the house renovated completely by then—maybe a second story? That would be amazing!

3. Write about how you see your relationship with people you love over the next year or two. What do you see your relationship with God looking like in the future? If you're a parent, write about you and your children as they grow and develop. Married? Dream about how you and your spouse will relate to one another in the future. Write about the things you'll be doing with your close friends. I would like to meet some new people, make new friends. I have wonderful old friends, but so many have moved away in the past few years. I would like to spend more time with my husband—be less busy and have quiet times with him. I would

like us to be able to talk more often about the things we want out of life. I hope to have a very open relationship with my kids. I want them to know they can talk to me about anything.

4. If you were to change one thing about your lifestyle, what would it be? Write about how this change would play out in your future and in your relationships in the future. I would change my addiction! I would get rid of it totally. It would mean *freedom* to me. I wouldn't have to feel ashamed or embarrassed when I meet new people—sometimes I feel my addiction causes me to hide away and not accomplish my dreams. I think I would be happier. I would be a better mother, too, because I don't want my kids to follow my example. I would have more money to spend on the renovations, vacations, and time away with my husband.

Now it's your turn:

1. What are you looking forward to doing in the next year or two?

_____

_____

_____

_____

_____

2. Write about your hopes and dreams for the future. Think about the next five years. What things will you be involved with? What interests will you be pursuing?

_____

_____

_____

_____

_____

3. Write about how you see your relationship with people you love over the next year or two. What do you see your relation-

ship with God looking like in the future? If you're a parent, write about you and your children as they grow and develop. Married? Dream about how you and your spouse will relate to one another in the future. Write about the things you'll be doing with your close friends.

_____

_____

_____

_____

_____

4. If you were to change one thing about your lifestyle, what would it be? Write about how this change would play out in your future and in your relationships in the future.

_____

_____

_____

_____

Once you're finished answering these questions, take a break. Spend some time doing other things, and allow the things you've written to simmer in the back of your mind. After your break (take no more than 24 hours), continue with the next exercise.

Weighing Your Thoughts

Maybe you've seen one of those "pros and cons" charts (maybe you've made one before), where on one side of a sheet of paper is a list of all the good things (the "pros") about a certain thing, and on the other side of the paper is a list of all the negative things (the "cons") about that same thing. It's a handy tool to use when trying to decide something big (like which house to buy or how you feel about the person who asked you out on a date). The exercise that follows is like the pros and cons charts, but it has a few important differences that make it the perfect tool to help you find that big arrow on your map that says "You Are Here."

To help you find yourself on your map, you need to ask yourself a question: "How do I feel about making some kind of change right now?"

Take a look at that question. Read it again. Notice that it says "some kind of change," not "a specific change." It's important not to jump ahead in the process, thinking you know exactly what change you want to make.

First, you need to know how you're really feeling about adding change to your life right now and how much change you really want to make. Also note that it says "right now." By completing the following exercise, you'll know how you feel about changing right now, and you'll have a good idea if your feelings will continue into the near future. This is important when embarking on a long-term change.

So clear your mind. Take a deep breath. Think only about the idea of making some kind of change in your life. Nothing specific— just the notion of making something change. Then you'll weigh your thoughts and know exactly how to proceed.

How to Weigh Your Thoughts

There are three parts to this self-exploration exercise. You most likely will be able to finish this exercise in <u>one sitting</u>, but it could take you longer than an hour. Also, it's possible you'll start this exercise, take a break from it, then return to finish it once you've given yourself more time to think about it. Either way, ensure that this exercise doesn't take longer than 24 hours. So, if you start working on this exercise at 7:00 P.M. tonight, you should be finished by 7:00 P.M. tomorrow.

First read the two statements at the top of the following chart. You'll see one that reads "What is good about *not changing* right now" and another that reads "What is good about *changing* right now." Choose which side you want to work on first. Then work only on that side until you've filled out the five lines under that heading. Ignore the scales for now.

So if you've decided to start with "What is good about *changing* right now," think only about the things you believe are positives about making some kind of a change at this time in your life. Fill out the five lines completely before you fill out the other side.

Remember: every answer is a good answer. I've filled out an example for you so you've an idea of what the chart could look like once it's filled out. Answer as honestly as you can. No one else is going to look at what you write; no one is judging your thoughts. Dig deep and be honest with yourself. It's the best way to know for certain that you're ready to take on making a change in your life.

Read the example. Then fill out the following blank chart with your answers. When you've finished filling out your answers, flip back to this page for instructions on how to use the scales.

On the Scales

Thoughts are funny things. If you have one, you're bound to have another, and then a whole bunch more follow. By now, you will have finished filling out the two main headings of the Weighing Your Thoughts chart. You have ten shiny thoughts: five *for* and five *against* the idea of making a change.

Another funny thing about thoughts: some of them are very heavy while others are light as air. The ideas you write down will not all be created equal. That's why you need to take the third and final step, which is to put your thoughts on the scales.

Each idea you'll write down will have an emotional or mental "weight" attached to it. It's possible that the way you feel about one idea on one side of the list will cause it to "weigh" more than all five ideas on the other side put together. It's just one reason, one idea, one thought, but it might mean more to you than the other reasons. Look at the example chart. You can see by looking at the numbers I've assigned each idea that the idea of "accomplishing something" weighs ten "pounds"—meaning it's very important and meaningful to me. On the other hand, "I have lots of stress in my life" on the "not changing" side, while true, rates only a five-pound weight.

Take a moment to "weigh" each idea you've written. Use a ten-pound scale. An idea that's less important to you *right now* is one pound. An idea that's moderately important to you *right now* will weigh five pounds. An idea that's very important to you *right now* will weigh ten pounds. Be sure that you rate each idea on its own and not in comparison to other ideas. Deal with each statement you've written, and choose a number based on how you feel, and think about that one statement alone.

When you've given each statement a weight, add up the "pounds" on each side of the list. Then write down the answer to the question that follows the chart. In the example, the scales add up as follows: Not changing right now = 31, Changing right now = 43. Therefore, in this case the answer is "Changing right now").

Weighing Your Thoughts Example

What is good about   What is good about
not changing right now   *changing* right now

It's easier not to change.	5	I would be accomplishing something.	10
My life is so busy already.	7	I think about making a change.	9
I can always make a change later.	7	I would feel stronger.	10

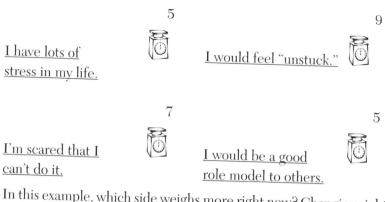

5

I have lots of
stress in my life.

9

I would feel "unstuck."

7

I'm scared that I
can't do it.

5

I would be a good
role model to others.

In this example, which side weighs more right now? Changing right now.

Now it's time for you to fill out the chart with your own answers. Refer back to the example if you need help. The instructions for how to use the scales are repeated at the bottom of this chart for ease of reference.

What is good about
not changing
right now

What is good about
changing right now

_____

_____

_____

_____

_____

_____

_____

_____

_____

_____

How to use the scales: Look at the lists you just created. Each idea you've written down has an emotional or mental "weight" attached to it. Take a moment to "weigh" each idea you've written down. Use a ten-pound scale. An idea that's less important to you right now is one pound. An idea that's moderately important to you right now will weigh five pounds. An idea that's very important to you right now will weigh ten pounds. Be sure that you rate each idea on its own and not based on comparison to other ideas. Deal with each statement you've written, and choose a number based on how you feel and think about that one statement alone.

When each statement has a weight, add up the pounds on each side of the list. Then write down the answer to the question that follows the chart.

Which side weighs more right now? _____

I Have My Number. Now What?

If the side for *making a change right now* weighs more than the *not making a change* side, then you're ready for some kind of a change in your life. Continue to chapter 7. If the side for *not making a change* weighs more than the other side, it will still be helpful for you to work through chapter 7. You'll do this scale again at the end of that chapter. Keep going! You'll learn more about your personal map toward change and be able to decide exactly what you want to do. In chapter 7 you'll be working toward discovering your do-able goals, which in turn will lead to your big goal.

Chapter 7

Identifying What Matters Most

Begin at the Beginning

Making a lifestyle change must begin at the beginning. Perhaps your answers to "Weighing Your Thoughts" in chapter 6 show you're ready to make a change. Now it's time to decide what to change. You probably have a general idea of the area of your life you want to see changes in. "I want to improve my health," "I want to gain control over my finances," "I want to have a happy marriage" are examples of typical general, large goals.

Goals like these are good starting places. They're the red flags along the way that point you in the right direction, but they don't tell your whole story.

You're going to learn how to break this large goal or outcome into smaller, "do-able" goals. A do-able goal is one that's *well defined* and therefore something you can achieve. You will choose your do-able goals based on your strengths and what's really important to you. If something is truly important to you, then you'll be able to make the change you want—and make it stick for life. Notice that I said it has to be something that's important to *you*, not something you think *should* be important, not something someone else told you should be important—important to *you*.

More of My Story

In chapter 6 I shared some of my story regarding my desire to lose weight. I told you that when I took time to reflect on my strengths and what I wanted out of life, I found out that weight loss wasn't my actual goal. It turned out that my desire to lose weight was only a step toward my true goal of having energy and being energetic. Losing weight was a *step* toward what I wanted. My goal was bigger than losing weight; in fact, losing weight was a smaller do-able goal in my process, which was also broken up into even smaller do-able goals.

Dare to live the life you have dreamed for yourself. Go forward and make your dreams come true (Ralph Waldo Emerson).

When I discovered my true goal, I stopped judging my progress by the scale. When I lost weight the first time around, I was a slave to the scale. My emotions would rise and fall with the numbers on the scale. After I discovered what was truly important to me, I was free to enjoy my journey, because my progress was no longer tied to a number on a scale. In time, I began to understand my body in new ways—its rhythms and cycles, its nutritional needs (never before had I actually craved salad!), as well as the needs for rest and for play. Discovering my true goal literally changed my life. I've learned to say "no" when I need to. I take time for myself. I smile more, and I enjoy my husband and family in new ways. I'm more productive at work. I'm full of energy. I'm friendlier. I'm happier.

Am I at my "ideal weight?" No; I still have a few pounds to go. Am I still working on that smaller goal? Yes. The difference for me is that now I'm enjoying the journey. I have a good attitude. I like myself the way I am even as I work toward getting to a different place. I've learned to mark my progress in positive ways and to thank God for all He has given me. There's joy in my journey.

There's fun and laughter, hope and joy for *you* in *your* journey, too. Are you ready to take the next step toward your joy-filled journey of change?

Finding Your Way

Think about the general goal you want to work toward. What's on your mind and heart?

Do you want to stop a behavior? For example, do you have an addiction you want to break, such as to cigarettes or alcohol? Do you engage in a habit you want to stop, such as looking at pornographic photos or films, gambling, or gossiping? Or maybe your large goal is to *start* doing something you believe would benefit you. Do you want to make new friends, read your Bible every day, or gain control over your finances? These are examples of general goals that involve starting a new behavior.

Maybe your general goal doesn't fit well into any of these categories. Is that goal to improve your marriage relationship? Get ahead at work? Be able to communicate more effectively with your mother-in-law? These are examples of large lifestyle goals.

Think about what's most important to you. You'll be using the "Finding My Way" chart to help you work out your true goal. The chart will help you move from thinking about your large, or general, goal (the outcome) to specific "do-able" goals. It's possible that you'll find you have several different large goals that are connected to each other in some way. That's fine. Write down each one as you think of it. The chart will also help you figure out what aspects of the large goal are important to you and which are not. It's going to help you "unpack" your large goal, examine its contents, and choose which things are truly meaningful to you.

For example, if you have a large goal to improve your health, you'll spend time thinking about what "improved health" looks like to you. The chart will help you understand which aspects of your life you think could be made "healthier." Dozens of health-related aspects of life could be improved: reduce stress, sleep better, lose weight, stop smoking, increase energy, enjoy sex more, or improve dental hygiene. The list is nearly endless.

You may look at the above list and think that every item on it sounds appealing. Yes, I would like to reduce my stress, sleep better, and lose weight! The question that needs to be answered is "What matters the most to me?" This is the key to finding out what your "do-able" goals are.

Don't worry about how you're going to accomplish your do-able goals. Concern yourself only with answering the question of which aspects of your large goal are important to you.

Use the example below as a guide to help you understand how to complete the chart.

How to use the "Finding My Way" chart

You'll probably need two separate sittings to complete this exercise. Fill out the first three columns first. This should take only a few minutes—no more than an hour. If you're able, move straight into filling out the last two columns. It may be, however, that you'll require as much or more time to fill out the last two columns as it took you to fill out the first three. If you can, walk away from the exercise and spend time thinking about your goals for a few hours; then come back and fill in the last two columns. Don't take longer than a day (24 hours) to complete this exercise.

On pages 90 and 91 you'll find an example of how the "Finding My Way" chart could be filled out. You'll see it's filled with question marks, uncertainty, and honesty. I didn't try to pretend to know all the answers. I didn't worry about what other people have said to me in the past or what they may think my goals should be. Instead, I spent time looking inside myself for my true thoughts and feelings. And then I wrote them down—uncensored.

Here's how I did it. First, I wrote my large goal under the column "General Goal." Next, I wrote what I thought that goal could look like in my life. I wrote down as many things as I could think of, putting each one in its own box under the column "What Does That Mean to Me?" I didn't spend time thinking everything through. I just wrote down what I thought as I thought it. By filling out this column, I came up with a whole bunch of "possible do-able goals." These are the smaller steps I'm taking on my way to the large goal.

Then, I moved to the next column on the right, "How Important Is This to Me?" I used the same number system as the one in the "Weighing My Thoughts" exercise, assigning each possible do-able goal a number based on how important I thought it was to me (1 being of very low importance, 10 being of the highest importance). You'll notice there are steps I didn't number because I really wasn't sure; it's okay if you don't have all the answers.

Then I moved to the next column, "How Do I Know It's Important?" For this I needed to think of a specific way to identify the possible goal's importance to me. Sometimes I was able to gage a possible goal's importance by my feelings when I thought about that goal. Sometimes I reflected on some behavior I was already doing that showed me that a certain possible do-able goal was important to me. Other times, I wasn't sure how important a goal was to me. When that happened, I simply wrote down that I wasn't sure. Then I left it alone and went to the next possible goal I had written.

My last step was to brainstorm ideas for the Possible "Do-able Goal" column. Here I thought about concrete things I could do in order to accomplish each possible goal. Write down your thoughts quickly. You'll spend time in chapter 8 looking at these ideas in greater detail. The main points of this exercise are to get your true thoughts and feelings down on paper and to begin generating ideas. Remember to use the exercises you did in previous chapters as guides to help you fill out this chart. Re-read your answers to the things you're looking forward to in life. Go over the "Weighing Your Thoughts" chart. Each exercise you've done is a stepping stone toward making a change in your life.

Finding My Way EXAMPLE CHART:

General Goal	What Does That Mean to Me?	How Important is This to Me? (1 to 10, 1 = not very important. 10 = very important.)	How Do I Know it's Important?	Possible "Do-able" Goal
Be healthier	Take better care of myself.	8	I think about what it would be like to have someone take care of me the way I take care of others.	I don't know. How do I stop the world and take a break?
	Take time off from all the busy "go-go-go."	10	Last week I stopped by a travel agency and looked at "spa get-away" packages.	Book the spa for a weekend? Maybe.
	Have more energy through the day.	9	I feel tired all the time.	Find out what could boost my energy levels. Maybe do some Internet research?
	Walk more.	6	I bought walking shoes last summer. I need to use them!	Go walking three times a week.

	Join a weight-loss group.	???	I'm not sure if this is what I want to do. But I have thought about it before.	This is a hard one for me. I'm not sure I'm ready to join a group. Maybe.
	Join a gym/ workout group.	?	I have thought about this before. I have a friend who just joined a gym.	Everyone goes to the gym these days. I could try it.
	Feel good about myself.	10	I really want to feel good about the way I look. I want to feel confident.	I need to work on not hating where I am just because I want to make some changes.
	Get outside more often.	9	I really love to be outside. I'm cooped up inside so much! I would love to be doing things outside!	I want to find ways to be outdoors more often. Maybe a project?

Now it's your turn.

Finding My Way

General Goal	What Does That Mean to Me?	How Important is This to Me? (1 to 10, 1 = not very important. 10 = very important.)	How Do I Know It's Important?	Possible "Do-able" Goal

So far in your journey toward change you've spent a good deal of time in self-reflection. You've identified some of your strengths. You've also taken time to think about your future and the things you're looking forward to. You've charted your possible do-able goals.

In the next chapter you'll begin to put the pieces together by examining the things you're already doing right. Then you'll learn how to apply your strengths to trying on possible do-able goals you've come up with in this chapter. Keep a bookmark here, as you'll be using your answers from this chapter to complete an exercise in chapter 8.

Chapter 8

Making Your Map

A friend of mine has a difficult relationship with her mother. She never knows where she stands with her mother from day to day. She's a grown woman with children of her own, but she feels caught in a game of "good girl, bad girl" with her mother. One day my friend blurted out to me, "I hate my mother!" We were both quiet for a while as we thought about her statement. Finally I said, "That's quite an insight."

She nodded, the full weight of her truth sinking in. It wasn't a pleasant truth, but it was her truth.

I asked, "What do you think you're going to do with that insight?"

She thought about it. "I don't *want* to hate her. God tells us that we have to honor our mother and father."

I smiled. "Do you think God is in the business of making unreasonable demands of us?"

Tears formed in her eyes. "No, I guess not. But—"

I interrupted. "In what way have you dishonored your mother?"

She looked at me as if I were daft. "I just said how! I hate her! I really do!"

"I heard that. But you've spent your entire life working to make things good between you and your mother. You've done everything she's ever asked of you. You tell her you love her nearly every day. Whenever she needs you, you're there.

The very least you can do in your life is to figure out what you hope for. And the most you can do is live inside that hope. Not admire it from a distance but live right in it, under its roof (Barbara Kingsolver).

You listen to her. When she lashes out, you're there to calm her down." I sat down beside her. "My friend, you've never done anything *but* honor your mother."

Like so many other people, she wasn't giving herself credit for the things she was doing *right*. She was focused on her "shortcomings"—the areas in which she believed she had "failed." She couldn't see all the good, right, praiseworthy, and loving things she had done. It didn't seem that it was good enough.

Have you ever felt the way my friend did? Focusing on the negative things, the supposed shortcomings? Have you been overlooking the positive things you've been doing right? When we overlook what we've been doing right, we forget that this is not the way God views our situation. And it's not the way He views us either. We cry out, *God! Come and help me in my problems!* Now, asking God for help is a good thing. Helpful. Necessary. However, prayers like this are incomplete.

Yes, we need help from God. But we also need to be able to take an honest and careful inventory of the help that He has already provided us through our strengths. It's important to give God credit and thanks for the good that has been happening even in the midst of difficult circumstances. When we do, we see the reality of God working in our lives.

Build on What You're Doing Right, Right Now

Look at your situation that you want to change (habit, bad relationship, whatever) and try to see the things you're *already doing right* in that situation or have tried in the past. Fill in the following chart, writing down every positive step you've taken toward making a change in your life. Do this exercise in one sitting, taking no more than 30 minutes or so. These are wonderful foundations for you to build your future successes on.

Spending time looking at the things you've done right is an act of self-love. God takes this seriously. Read Matthew 22:36-40. Jesus tells us that the entire law of God is about love—love for God, others, and yourself.

Spending time looking at the things you've done right is also an act of worship to God. When we look back with the intention of seeing what went right, we're giving God credit for the good things He has done in our lives. We're thanking Him. We're recognizing Him for who He is. It's a wonderful thing to do. You'll be encouraged.

Begin by filling out the column "What I'm doing right." Any positive step you've tried (even if you think, *It didn't work in the end*) should be included—big things and little things. Include things you've done and things you've thought, ideas you've had or tried, or times you felt inspired.

Next, decide how well each positive step worked for you by using the same number system as before: 1 = the step was not very effective, 10 = the step was very effective. Then reflect on these steps you've taken by thinking about which strengths you used when you tried them. What was the driving force behind your positive steps? What was the motivation? What was inspiring you to take the step? Asking these questions will help you figure out which strengths you were using at the time you took the positive step.

Follow the example given to help you see how the chart might look filled out. The example uses the situation of my friend and her mother.

What I'm doing right	How well this worked for me 1= not well 10= very well	Strengths I'm using to do things right
I'm still talking to my mother.	7	I love my family, and I want my children to have a good relationship with their grandmother.
I try to tell my mother that I love her every time I talk to/see her.	9	I care about other people's feelings.
I give myself breaks now and then from her frequent phone calls (voice mail/just don't answer the phone).	10	I love to be outside, so I go for walks or go in the yard and let the voice mail answer calls for the afternoon. Or I go out with a friend.
I have asked my husband to talk to my mother a few times.	6	I'm letting my husband take care of me a little bit, when I ask him to take over with my mom.
I have tried to see her for who she is.	2	I don't know which strength I've used here. It actually hasn't worked that well, because I see her as my mom, and I can't seem to get past that.
I tell myself that I'm an adult now and don't have to act like her "child."	5	I use my critical thinking skills. It's reasonable for me to "act my age" and not react to her as if I were a child.
I talk to friends about my feelings about my mother.	8	I love my friends. I find what I like best is when my friends just listen to me and don't judge me.

Now it's your turn. Look at your situation, habit, or addiction in terms of the things you are already doing right or that you have tried in the past and they worked well for you, even if only for a short time. Even though you haven't fixed your situation or kicked your habit or addiction yet, you've still done things that have moved you in the right direction. These are successes you can build on.

What I'm doing right	How well this worked for me 1= not well 10= very well	Strengths I'm using to do things right

Map Making

In the previous chapter you spent time thinking about possible do-able goals based on the things that are most important to you. In this chapter you'll be "trying on" these possible goals using your strengths.

There are two ways you'll be using your strengths to try on your possible do-able goals. The first way is by "trying on" new ways of thinking. The second is "trying on" new behaviors.

Thinking Matters

Changing a behavior sometimes begins with changing your mind.

Jim was in the middle of a messy, angry divorce. He was hurting, missing his daughter, and furious with his estranged wife. "I can't forgive her," he said to me over and over. But his unforgiveness was chewing a hole in his soul. He went from being an easygoing guy to an uptight, short-tempered man. He felt miserable most of the time.

He asked me if there was a way he could stop feeling so bad while still not forgiving his wife. We talked about it—could it be done? After a while I asked him, "What do you really want out of life? What's really important to you?" He had a long list of wonderful things that were important to him. I asked him to spend time thinking about those wonderful hopes before we met again. I asked him to talk to God about those dreams and hopes. Notice that I didn't ask him to talk to God about the terrible feelings or his inability to forgive his wife. The next time I saw him, he said, "I'm ready to stop feeling miserable all the time. I'm ready to see what it takes to make that happen."

He was on the road to forgiving his estranged wife. He was beginning to change his mind about hanging on to years of anger. He didn't get on the road to forgiveness by changing what he was doing; he began by changing his thinking, and that opened his heart to God. His life was transformed. Romans 12:1-2 talks about the process of changing our lives by opening ourselves up to God. It begins with a willingness to accept God's mercy, offering our lives up to Him, and allowing Him to change our minds about how we had been living.

Our thinking affects our actions. How we think about a behavior, or about changing a behavior, affects what we actually do. Philippians 2:5-7 talks about the limitless depth of goodness that can come out of having a positive attitude. Jesus had this attitude, and He changed the world.

If you're feeling stuck in a rut—for example, you really want to spend more time with your family than at work, but you regularly find yourself at the office well into the evening—then changing your thinking about your situation will help you to change the actual behavior.

You're going to be using your strengths to help you try on new ways of thinking about what you want to change. You're also going to be asking God for specific help in doing this.

In the Change Room

Most of us have tried on clothes in a change room at a store. First, you spend time browsing the selection of clothes, then take some articles into the change room to try on. Some clothes don't fit—either they're too big or too small—so you put them aside and try on the next article of clothing you brought in.

Sometimes you try on something and it fits you, but you're not certain you like it. You need to spend time looking at the cut, considering how the material hangs on your frame, and deciding if it's comfortable. Sometimes you need to come out of the change room and show a friend or a sales clerk and ask his or her opinion. Then you make up your mind as to whether it's going to work for you—if you like it.

Then there are those rare, magical moments when you try something on and "wow"—it fits, it feels great, and you look fantastic. But you never would have known if you hadn't tried it on.

Using Your Strengths in the Change Room

When you go shopping for new clothes, you don't walk into a store and ask to try on everything. Instead, you browse through and choose articles you think you like and will look good on you. You reject the things you don't like or believe aren't flattering.

That's how your strengths will work for you in this part of the process. They'll guide your choices, helping you know which things to try on. You'll hold up a new behavior and compare it to your list of strengths. If it lines up with something you love, something you're good at, something that inspires you, then you'll put it in your change room to try on. You'll do the same thing with a new thought or attitude.

Just like trying on clothes, trying on new thoughts and behaviors can sometimes be uncomfortable. I can recall a time I thought a pair of jeans I was trying on really *should* fit me, even though they were clearly too small for me. I fought with them for a long time until I realized I was exhausted, and, even worse—I was stuck in the jeans! You can avoid my mistake by doing two important things: use your strengths as a guide to what to try on, and use prayer as your mirror to help you see if what you're trying becomes you.

The Mirror of Prayer

Prayer is important to the process of change. We've talked about how God has been with you from the very beginning and how He's with you now as you map out your journey. For this part of the process, prayer is your mirror. It's what you look into to help you see if what you're trying on fits, hangs right, and is comfortable. Why prayer?

Prayer connects you to God. When you pray you're speaking with the One who created you. He knows you best—better than you know yourself. As you spend time talking with God, He is speaking back to you, affirming His love for you, revealing new facets of your strengths, and showing you wonderful things about Him and about you. Prayer changes you. Second Corinthians 3:17-18 talks about seeing, as if looking in a mirror, how God changes us in exciting ways to be more like Him.

When prayer is your mirror, you're able to see yourself as God sees you: blessed, capable, loved, and important, filled with good things from God. When you ask God about your progress and your journey, you aren't going to be discouraged. You'll be encouraged, strengthened, filled with hope and the knowledge that you can succeed with God's help. In fact, God has even bigger things in store for you as you walk with Him. Read 1 Corinthians 1:26-31 for just a hint of the wonderful things God has for you.

In the next exercise, you're going to learn how to combine your strengths with prayer and your possible do-able goals in the change room of your life. Keep the prayers short if you can; that way you'll have no trouble remembering to pray them throughout the day.

In the previous chapter, you wrote down several possible goals based on things that are truly important to you. Now, you'll take those goals and think of specific things you can do to try the goal on. This will help you see what specific aspects of the goal are important to you. You'll try the goals on by trying out new ways of thinking and new behaviors. You'll be using different strengths to help you "try on" what it's like to be the person who has already made the lifestyle change you're thinking about.

For example, maybe one of your possible do-able goals is to have control over your temper, and you've discovered you have the strength of curiosity about the world. You'll combine these two things to come up with new ways of thinking and behaving that you can try on. Maybe you'll try on new ways of thinking by asking yourself questions about what it would be like to live in a world where you had control over your temper. What would this new world look like? What would you be doing? What would it feel like? How would things be different for you? By asking these kinds of questions, you would be trying on new ways of thinking about your situation.

For the sake of our example, let's say you've also discovered you have the strength of a sense of humor. You would use this strength to help you come up with new ways to think or behave in order to try on the goal of controlling your temper. You might decide to initiate a conversation with a person at work who normally rubs you the wrong way, and then use your sense of humor to help you remain in control of your temper by defusing tense moments through sharing a funny story or an appropriate joke.

List your strengths on the space below. It can be the same list of strengths you listed earlier or, if you've already discovered new strengths, you can include them in this list. Remember: five strengths is just the starting point. Don't feel you should only list and work with five of your strengths if you've discovered more.

After you've listed your strengths, read the instructions on how to use the "Trying On My Strengths" chart. I've filled out an example chart with ideas of how this chart could be filled out.

Take a moment to remind yourself of your strengths. If you would like to, try writing down as many of them as you can without looking back at the previous chapter. This will help you reinforce your strengths in your mind.

My Strengths: 1. _____

2. _____

3. _____

4. _____

5. _____

The following chart can be done in one sitting. Try to fill in as much as you can in one sitting. If you need to take a break to think things through, try not to take more than a few hours so that you can fill out the chart by the end of the day. That way you'll be able to begin trying on new thoughts and behaviors right away.

You'll be working with this chart for the next two weeks. It's possible that in that time you'll revisit and revise this chart based on new ideas you've had as you've tried on new thinking and behavior. It's not as if you *must* do something because you wrote it down. This takes practice. You'll be planning *your* path. Give yourself the time you need to chart your course. And allow yourself the space to change your mind if that's what happens.

Work through the example below before beginning the blank worksheet. Notice that different strengths can be used for one goal. Also notice how different goals can use the same strengths.

The example below is taken from the example in chapter 7. It's been filled out only as a guide to show you how the chart works.

Trying on My Strengths Example Chart:

Possible do-able goal	My Strength	How I can use it	How I can use it	How I can use it	How I can use it	Prayer
Take a break.	Creativity	Leave the building during my coffee breaks at work.	Read a book about how to take breaks.	Make time for my favorite hobby.	Write a list of things that are my definition of "break."	Help me, Lord, to be a human being, not always a human "doing."

Boost my energy levels.	Critical thinking and judgment	Plan my days so that I have time devoted to working out.	Talk to a doctor or nutritionist about foods that help increase energy.	Get a checkup and talk to the doctor about my low energy levels.	Get more sleep!	Thanks for the mind you gave me. Help me to use it well.
Go walking/get outside more often.	Humor	Challenge my kids to a walk-a-thon: prizes for the "funniest walker."	Leave important papers in the car so I have to keep going outside to get them for work.	Offer to walk my neighbors' huge, slobbery dog for them.	Ask the paper boy to leave the newspaper at the end of the driveway so I have to walk to get it!	Help me to find joy in the world you created.
Join a weight-loss group/start losing weight.	Daydreaming/planning	I can daydream about the life I want.	I can buy an outfit in the size I want to be.	I can write a list of all the healthful foods I like to eat.	Go online and find out what to expect at a group meeting.	Lord, be with me in my daydreams. Be with me in my planning.
Join a gym/start working out.	Love of family and friends	I can ask my spouse to encourage me as I figure out the best way to work out.	Make a "workout date" with my daughter once a week.	Ask a friend to join a local gym with me.	Think about the things I would like to do with my family but don't have the energy right now.	My body is a temple of the Holy Spirit. Help me to value my body as you do.
Love myself more (better image of self).	Daydreaming/planning	Practice what I would say in social situations.	Daydream about myself living the life I want to live.	Read a book about improving self-image.	Write down the things I do that are valuable and important.	Help me understand how you love me, so I can love me too.

Now it's your turn:

Start by filling in the first column of your possible do-able goals (the lefthand side of the chart). You'll find your possible goals in the chart you filled out in chapter 7. If you think of other possible goals you want to try, include them in this chart.

Then in the column beside each possible do-able goal, list one of your strengths. To the right of that column, you'll write down four different ways you can use your strength to "try on" the possible goal. Sometimes you'll write down a new way of thinking to try on; other times you'll write down a new behavior you can try on. To the right of those four ideas, write down a prayer about your possible goal. Search your heart and mind for what you really want to say to God about the possible goal. Be open with Him. Your prayer could be asking God to help you, or it could be a prayer of thanksgiving. It can be a passage from the Bible that inspires you, or a prayer sharing your fears and frustrations with God. You can use a prayer you've heard before or one you make up on your own. The point is to remember that you're not alone as you journey toward change. God is with you. If possible, keep your prayer short so it's easy to remember and pray at different times of the day. If you find that sticking to one prayer for each goal doesn't work for you, or if there are other ways you like to pray, then just jot down the main ideas, desires, hopes, and so on, that you plan to pray about.

On the next row, write down a second possible goal, a strength (it can be the same one as you used in for the first possible goal, or it can be a different one), and four ways to try on the possible goal using the specific strength. Then, write a short prayer about that possible goal. Keep going until you've written down all the possible goals that you want to try on.

Each strength you use and every idea you try is a step toward helping you know which goals is important to you. You can add to your list of possible goals as often as you like, but be sure you finish trying on the ideas you've already written down.

Trying on My Strengths

Possible do-able goal	My strength	How I can use it	How I can use it	How I can use it	How I can use it	Prayer

In the chart above (Trying on My Strengths) you drafted possible paths in your journey of change by brainstorming possible do-able goals and new ways of thinking and behaving using your strengths. Now it's time to actually begin trying on the new thinking and behaviors.

Change means disruption of routine. This isn't a negative thing; I've heard it said that change can be as refreshing as a vacation. I like this analogy. Every time I've gone on vacation, I've had plenty of disruption (packing into suitcases nearly everything I own, finding someone to take care of the cat, canceling the newspaper, herding a family of four through airports and strange cities), but it's been a pleasant disruption. I welcomed it, because I was excited about my destination.

That's how I hope you view the disruptions that are sure to come your way as you journey toward discovering your true goal. It's an exciting time, because the destination is thrilling.

Journaling My Journey

This exercise is different from previous ones in that it's *on-going*. You'll be referring to it several times over the two weeks or so that you're trying on goals. I suggest keeping it in a private place (perhaps beside your bed or in the same place you keep your personal journal if you have one). When you have time, reflect on your experiences, and try on new thoughts and behaviors and write about them. Each session with the journal will be as long or as short as you want it to be.

Read over your chart below, and decide on a specific amount of time that you'll give yourself to try on the new ways of thinking and behaving. It should be no more than two weeks. You'll be using your completed "Trying on My Strengths" chart along with this exercise.

Check off each new way of thinking and behaving from your "Trying on My Strengths" chart as you complete it. Some of the things you'll be trying on are one-time efforts. For example, one of my ideas was to write a list of all the healthful foods I enjoy eating. That's a one-time behavior. Other things require an ongoing effort in order to really try them on. For example, I wrote "leave the building during coffee breaks." This requires an ongoing effort in order to fully "try it on." I'll need to do it repeatedly over time to see if it's going to work for me.

You can try on new ways of thinking and new behaviors simultaneously—you don't have to do them one at a time. To help you keep track of your journey, use the "Journaling My Journey" chart below to keep track of your progress. As you try on new thoughts and behaviors, write about your experience. Begin by writing down your possible do-able goals (take them from the "Trying on My Strengths" chart). Then write down the strengths you used to try on the possible do-able goal. Then, as you go, jot down what you did, and your reaction. Did you enjoy it? How did it make you feel?

Under that, write about how trying on the new thought or behavior helped you decide about that specific possible do-able goal.

Were you able to see that this goal is the right one for you? Write it down. Did you find the goal wasn't what you hoped it would be? Write about that experience. Use the following example to help you understand how to complete this exercise. Then write about your unique journey on the blank form.

Remember: you're just trying things on. There's no way you can "fail" at this. Think of this time as being in the changing room, trying on different "clothes." Some fit; some don't. Some look good; some are not your style.

How Did It Go?
Journaling My Journey Example:

Possible do-able Goal: Weight loss/Join a weight-loss group

Prayer: God, thank you for giving me the ability to see things in a new way. Help me to see all my capabilities!

The strengths I used: Creativity and humor

How I did it: I found an old picture of me from my "skinny" days. I put it on the fridge. Then I made a collage for my fridge! I found pictures of veggies and fruit and other healthful food. I pasted them together on a big roll of paper. On top of that I pasted the words "Choose Us First!" I put the whole thing on my fridge. Now, when I walk into the kitchen, I see a fun reminder to grab a healthful snack first!

How it helped me decide about this goal: Trying out this goal was great, because it got me thinking about all the healthful foods I really like. There are more than I realized! After I finished the collage I went online and found healthful recipes that include the foods I like. I know now that I can make weight loss fun, and having fun is really important to me.

Possible do-able Goal: Take a break

Prayer: Rest is important for my health. Help me to relax and enjoy the journey.

The strengths I used: Daydreaming/planning and my love for my family.

How I did it: One evening I took a long bubble bath and day-dreamed about the life I want. I saw myself doing all kinds of things—lots of them are things I do already. The difference for me was that as I was doing things I enjoy, I wasn't feeling rushed or hurried. I was feeling that I could take my time and enjoy the activity. After that, I talked to my family about my daydream—how I was feeling—and I asked them how they were feeling. It was amazing! All of us have been feeling rushed and too busy.

How it helped me deicide about this goal: Talking to my family was a real eye-opener for me. As we talked, we began to see we all needed to slow down. We are working on a plan as a family on what activities to pare down or stop altogether. I also realized that it's the feeling of being rushed, hurried, and pushed that bothers me most.

Possible do-able Goal: Join a gym/work-out group

Prayer: Thank you for my friends!

The strengths I used: Love of family and friends and planning

How I did it: I asked a friend to come with me to the gym, just to try it out. It was great to have her with me, because I didn't feel alone. I tried different equipment and even joined a half-hour aerobics class.

How it helped me decide about this goal: I'm so glad I went to the gym to see what happens there and how things work. It helped me understand that the gym isn't going to work for me right now. Even having my friend with me, I wasn't comfortable enough to feel that I wanted to go back. Instead, two of my friends are joining me three times a week to do a workout on our own with videos from the library! I'm excited about this!

How Did It Go?
Journaling the Journey

Write down your possible goals (take them from the "Trying on My Strengths" chart). Then write down the strengths you used to try on the possible goal. Each time you try on a new thought or behavior, jot down what you did and your reaction. Did you enjoy it? How did it make you feel?

Under that, write about how trying on the new thought or behavior helped you decide about that specific possible goal. Were you able to see how this goal is the right one for you? Write it down. Did you find the goal wasn't what you hoped it would be? Write about that experience.

Possible do-able goal: _____

Prayer: _____

_____

_____

_____

_____

The strengths I used: _____

_____

_____

_____

_____

How I did it: _____

_____

_____

_____

_____

How it helped me decide about this goal: _____

_____

_____

_____

_____

———

Possible do-able goal: _____

Prayer: _____

_____

_____

_____

_____

The strengths I used: _____

_____

_____

_____

_____

How I did it: _____

_____

_____

_____

_____

How it helped me decide about this goal: _____

_____

_____

_____

_____

———

Possible do-able goal: _____

Prayer: _____

_____

_____

_____

The strengths I used: _____

_____

_____

_____

How I did it: _____

_____

_____

_____

_____

How it helped me decide about this goal: _____

_____

_____

_____

_____

———

Possible do-able goal: _____

Prayer: _____

_____

_____

_____

The strengths I used: _____

_____

_____

_____

How I did it: _____

_____

_____

_____

How it helped me decide about this goal: _____

_____

_____

_____

_____

———

Possible do-able goal: _____

Prayer: _____

_____

_____

_____

The strengths I used: _____

_____

_____

_____

How I did it: _____

_____

_____

_____

How it helped me decide about this goal: _____

_____

_____

_____

_____

Keep working through the process of trying on new ways of thinking and behaving. If you try something and find you don't like it or it doesn't seem to work for you, leave it—don't force yourself to see it through to the bitter end. If something doesn't work for you, that's okay! Not everything you think of will be a perfect fit. Just keep using your strengths to try things on, and you'll find many "perfect fits."

In the next chapter you'll be putting all your hard work toward pinpointing your exact long-term goal. This will be your true goal, based on what is important to you, and you'll be using your strengths to achieve it.

Chapter 9

The Long-term Goal

Gains Made

As you've worked through this book, you've made tremendous gains! You've accomplished important things in every aspect of your life as you've journeyed through change. Take time to think and reflect on all you've accomplished so far, and you'll find there is no aspect of your life that you haven't improved since you began this journey.

Most likely, you'll be able to finish this exercise in one sitting in less than one hour. If you need to take a break from it and then come back to finish later, be sure to finish it the same day you started it. This exercise is meant to be a pat on the back, an encouragement that will give you a boost as you continue your journey. I've included an example to help you see how these questions could be answered. Remember: your answers are unique to your journey.

Gains Examples:

Write down some of the important gains you've made in your life so far on this journey.

1. **Gains I have made in my physical and mental health.** I have a better sense of what is important to me. I now understand my goal is made up of smaller steps that I can actually take. I feel better about who I am and my ability to change. I understand God loves me. I've always known that, but by asking God to show me my strengths and how they work, I think I better understand how much He loves me.

2. **Gains I have made in my home life.** I'm better able to speak up and ask for the things I need from my husband and even from my kids. My husband has been asking questions about using his strengths, and we've talked about ourselves and our hopes and dreams in ways that we haven't done since we first were married.

3. **Gains I have made in my self-confidence.** I understand now that's it's okay to love myself *the way I am*. I don't need to wait until everything is "perfect" before I can love myself. I'm beginning to see that I'm made up of good stuff—strengths. I'm also beginning to feel that maybe God isn't mad at me but that He planned me from the beginning and is involved in my life.

4. **Gains I have made in my plans for the future.** I've had goals before, but for the first time I'm actually excited about my goals! I know I can achieve them. God has given me the tools I need, and I'm exploring different ways to use them. It's thrilling to know—really know—that I can do this!

5. **Gains I have made in my relationship with God.** I feel closer to God than I did before I started. I pray more often now. I see that prayer doesn't always mean a long time alone on my knees but that I can speak to God whenever—I'm feeling more connected to Him.

Now it's your turn to think about the wonderful gains you've made in your journey so far. This is a pleasant and life-affirming thing to do. It's not boasting or being vain or proud. It's celebrating the amazing life God has given you.

Gains:

Write down some of the important gains you've made in your life so far on this journey.

1. Gains I have made in my physical and mental health.

_____

_____

_____

_____

_____

_____

2. Gains I have made in my home life.

_____

_____

_____

_____

_____

_____

3. Gains I have made in my self-confidence.

_____

_____

_____

_____

_____

4. Gains I have made in my plans for the future.

_____

_____

_____

_____

_____

5. Gains I have made in my relationship with God.

_____

_____

_____

_____

_____

X Marks the Spot

This is a quick exercise and will likely take you less than 30 minutes.

In chapter 6 you daydreamed about your future and wrote about the things you're looking forward to in the next one to five years. You also wrote about your important relationships. Look back on your responses to those questions. Reflect on them, and add to them if you like. Then take a moment to answer the following questions:

1. How do you see the role a lifestyle change will play in your future and in your relationships in the future?

_____

_____

_____

_____

_____

2. What changes would you like to make that would positively affect your life? (Be as specific as you can. Look back at your "How Did It Go?" chart for specific goals.)

_____

_____

_____

_____

_____

The Destination

The following exercise can be done in an hour or less. It's possible you may need two sessions to complete the chart. If so, take no more than 24 hours to complete the entire chart.

For this exercise you'll use your "Journaling My Journey" answers to complete the chart. In much the same way as you pulled patterns from your "understanding journal" in chapter 4, you'll find the answer to your true long-term goal in your "Journaling My Journey" exercise.

No smile is as beautiful as the one that struggles through tears (anonymous).

To complete the chart, write down your possible do-able goals from your "Journaling My Journey" exercise in chapter 8. Then write down all the strengths you used when you tried on the possible do-able goals. Make a note of what you actually did (which may differ from what you wrote down in chapter 8—that's fine; just note the things you actually did).

Last, summarize how you think it went. Think about the efforts you made and the things you discovered about the goal and yourself. Note any changes you made to your goal or to what you actually did to try on the goal. Make note of any important interaction you had with family or friends or other people who support you in your changes. Take your time on this last column, as the information you write in it will be important as you decide your long-term goal. The example here uses the example answers from chapter 8.

Pulling Patterns from Journaling My Journey

Possible do-able goal	Strengths used	What I did	How it worked
Weight loss/join a weight-loss group.	Creativity/Humor	Created a fun reminder to eat well and posted an old picture of myself on the fridge.	I took the picture down. I felt that I was comparing myself to my "younger" self, and I didn't like it. I kept the veggie picture up. I like it!
Take a break.	Daydreaming/ planning/love of family and friends	Daydreamed about the life I want. Talked to my family.	We've made *huge* changes by making *small* changes to everyone's schedules. We talk more as a family, and we plan more things together, which makes life better for all of us!
Join a gym/ workout group.	Love of family and friends/planning	Asked a friend to join me at the gym. Started working out with friends.	It's difficult for my friends and me to get together every week. We're all so busy. We've tried, but it's too much juggling schedules. I need to rethink my workout goal.

Now it's your turn to pull patterns from your journal. Fill in the chart below. Take as much time as you need to reflect on the important things you discovered about yourself and about each possible do-able goal. If it comes to mind, jot it down.

Pulling Patterns from Journaling My Journey

Possible do-able goal	Strengths used	What I did	How it worked

Now it's time to find your true long-term goal. To do this, you will examine your completed chart (above). This exercise will take you more than an hour to complete. It will be most helpful if you can finish it in one sitting, but if you need to break it up, try to complete it in two sittings on the same day or in a 24-hour period at the most. You will be working on your chart and answering questions about your chart in this exercise.

To begin, examine the strengths you used to try on each possible do-able goal. Which strength(s) did you use the most often? (In the example, strengths of planning and love for family and friends were used most often.)

Then examine your answers to "How it Worked." Look for patterns, beginning with changes you made along the way. I've included in the following chart examples of how to find changes:

Possible do-able goal	Strengths used	What I did	How it worked
Weight loss/join a weight-loss group.	Creativity/ Humor	Created a fun reminder to eat well and posted an old picture of myself on the fridge.	I took the picture down. I felt that I was comparing myself to my "younger" self, and I didn't like it. I kept the veggie picture up. I like it!
Take a break.	Daydreaming/ planning/love of family and friends	Daydreamed about the life I want. Talked to my family.	We've made *huge* changes by making *small* changes to everyone's schedules. We talk more as a family, and we plan more things together, which makes life better for all of us!
Join a gym/workout group.	Love of family and friends/ planning	Asked a friend to join me at the gym. Started working out with friends.	It's difficult for my friends and me to get together every week. We're all so busy. We've tried, but it's too much juggling schedules. I need to rethink my workout goal.

There are changes that occurred in every section in this example. This is typical of most people's experience. Rarely do the things we plan go exactly as we thought they might. That's the purpose of trying them on, to see how the reality stacks up against the idea. Look for change statements in your chart; then answer the questions about them in the following exercise.

Next, take a look at the patterns involving your feelings about the things you tried on. Below are examples of feelings and emotions that are shaded.

Possible do-able goal	Strengths used	What I did	How it worked
Weight loss/join a weight-loss group.	Creativity/ Humor	Created a fun reminder to eat well and posted an old picture of myself on the fridge.	I took the picture down. I felt that I was comparing myself to my "younger" self, and I didn't like it. I kept the veggie picture up. I like it!
Take a break.	Daydreaming/ planning/love of family and friends	Daydreamed about the life I want. Talked to my family.	We've made *huge* changes by making *small* changes to everyone's schedules. We talk more as a family, and we plan more things together, which makes life better for all of us!
Join a gym/ workout group.	Love of family and friends/planning	Asked a friend to join me at the gym. Started working out with friends.	It's difficult for my friends and me to get together every week. We're all so busy. We've tried, but it's too much juggling schedules. I need to rethink my workout goal.

Feeling statements don't always include an emotion, but they are tied to our emotions. For example, "juggling schedules" is an activity, but in this example there are feelings attached to it that are strong enough to warrant rethinking the goal. Look for feeling and emotion statements in your chart, and then answer the questions about them in the exercise below.

Last, look for patterns regarding things that worked well for you and that you enjoyed. Below are examples of statements that show goals that worked well.

Possible do-able goal	Strengths used	What I did	How it worked
Weight loss/join a weight-loss group.	Creativity/ Humor	Created a fun reminder to eat well and posted an old picture of myself on the fridge.	I took the picture down. I felt that I was comparing myself to my "younger" self, and I didn't like it. I kept the veggie picture up. I like it!
Take a break.	Daydreaming/ planning/love of family and friends	Daydreamed about the life I want. Talked to my family.	We've made *huge* changes by making *small* changes to everyone's schedules. We talk more as a family, and we plan more things together, which makes life better for all of us!
Join a gym/ workout group.	Love of family and friends/planning	Asked a friend to join me at the gym. Started working out with friends.	It's difficult for my friends and me to get together every week. We're all so busy. We've tried, but it's too much juggling schedules. I need to rethink my workout goal.

Above, we see there are things that worked very well, and there are things that didn't fit. I ignored the statements that talked about what didn't work and focused only on what worked well. Look in your chart for statements that talk about what worked. Then answer the questions about them in the exercise.

Use the following example to help you understand how you could fill out the questions.

Finding My Long-term Goal

1. Which strengths did you use most often? Planning, and love for family and friends.

2. What changes did you make to your original ideas? I took down the "skinny me" picture. Changes were made in the whole family's schedules, not just my own, and I decided to rethink my workout goal.

3. What feelings and emotions did you experience? I didn't like the "skinny me" picture. It was taken years ago—I felt as if I were trying to become "young" again, and that's not what I want. I want to be the best me today. I feel relief and happiness about my family dropping some of our outside activities. I feel that life is better for us. When it came to working out, I felt overwhelmed at the gym, but trying to get together with friends to work out was frustrating. I'm feeling uncertain about that goal.

4. What worked best for you? The veggie picture was fun to do, and when I look at it I feel that sense of fun, so it really helps me to remember to eat better. Dropping some of the activities my family was involved in worked amazingly well. It was the best change for me!

Now it's your turn to answer these questions. Take your time and fill in any extra ideas, thoughts, or experiences you recall even if they don't appear on your chart.

Finding My Long-term Goal

1. Which strengths did you use most often?

_____

_____

_____

_____

_____

2. What changes did you make to your original ideas?

_____

_____

_____

_____

3. What feelings and emotions did you experience?

_____

_____

_____

_____

4. What worked best for you?

_____

_____

_____

_____

From the example answers in the charts, I've pulled out the long-term goal. You'll recall the original large goal for this individual was to "take better care of myself." Based on the different things that were "tried on" and the responses to the questions, I was able to discover the true long-term goal. What would you say the long-term goal for this individual is? The words you used were probably different, but it would be something along the line of— Spend more focused time at home with my family, making them the priority instead of filling my life with outside activities.

The change you're going to make is for a *long-term* goal. This means it's something you're going to work toward. You won't get to your long-term goal in one giant leap. It takes smaller steps. In the space below write down your *long-term* goal. Long-term goals could be—quit smoking, or cut down on the number of cigarettes I smoke; socialize twice a week with people from work; spend at least 30 minutes a day exercising. They are long-term, but they are specific. Look at your answers and decide on your true long-term goal.

My Long-term Goal:

_____

_____

_____

_____

You'll learn how to apply your strengths to your long-term goal as you work through the rest of this book.

Now that you have a specific goal that you'll be working toward, it's time to revisit the "Weighing Your Thoughts" exercise from chapter 6. You'll recall when you first did this exercise you were simply thinking about making some sort of change in your life.

This time when you fill out the "Weighing Your Thoughts" exercise, have your specific goal in mind. Think about what is good about *not* making this specific change in your life and what is good about making it. Try to do the exercise in one sitting, taking less than 30 minutes.

"Weighing Your Thoughts" Example

This example is for the specific goal of "I want to stop gossiping about others and having negative thoughts about others."

What is good about *not* making this this specific change	What is good about making this specific change

7

It affects my social
life.

10

I'm ready to feel
better about myself.

5

Friends don't always
understand.

8

I can see the good in
others when I try.

4

I don't always know
what to say.

8

I want to be liked
by other people.

5

Changing is difficult
sometimes.

8

I like myself when
I'm not being negative.

3

I sometimes think of
giving up.

9

I would be a good
role model to my kids.

Which side weighs more right now?

Weighing Your Thoughts

What is good about
not making this
specific change

What is good about making
this specific change

_____

_____

_____

_____

_____   _____

_____   _____

_____   _____

How to use the scales: Look at the lists you just created. Each idea you've written down has an emotional or mental "weight" attached to it. Sometimes the way we feel or think about one idea on one side of the list will cause it to "weigh" more than five ideas on the other side just because of how we feel or think about it.

Take a moment to "weigh" each idea you've written down. Use a 10-pound scale. An idea that's less important to you right now is one pound. An idea that's moderately important to you right now will weigh five pounds. An idea that's very important to you right now will weigh 10 pounds.

Write down the "weight" of each statement you recorded. Then add up the pounds on both sides of the list. Which side weighs more right now? _____

Take a moment to look back on the numbers from the previous "Weighing Your Thoughts" exercise. Compare how you were feeling about making a change then to how you feel about it now. Take a moment to reflect on how using your strengths helped you try on different possible goals and how you used your strengths to choose your long-term goal.

Is there a difference between the weights of this list compared to the list you completed earlier? What is the difference? _____

Walking Toward the Goal

Your goal is a *long-term* goal—something you're working toward at a pace of change you're comfortable with. No one is asking you to accomplish your long-term goal overnight, and no one is asking you to do something you honestly don't believe you can do right now.

You've already made several important steps toward your goal. If you look back at the work you've done, you'll see the road of change you've been walking already. That is the nature of change. It's not usually a "one thing at a time" experience. It's often a "several things at once" over-time experience. That's why you spent time looking at thoughts, feelings, and behaviors, because change can happen on any or all of these levels at the same time.

As you move forward on your map, it's important to remember that you're in charge. You decide the best path to take that will move you toward your goal. Sometimes this is straightforward. For example, even though I'm a loving mom of two young children, I know that working as a leader in children's ministry at church is not one of my strengths. I'm not cut out for it. Seriously, I'm a mess at it. It's hysterical to watch me even try. But that's fine with me. I don't have to be a super children's ministry person. My strengths are elsewhere. At the same time, I'm a good helper. Tell me what to do, and I'm off and running. Just *please* don't ask me to plan the lessons. They'll be dull.

Other times, you'll find that you can actually be *doing* the exact same behavior you have tried in the past, but now it works for you. For example, I told you about my weight-loss journey. The first time I lost weight, I joined a well-known weight-loss group, and while I dropped pounds, I didn't actually change. All I did was follow a list of behaviors that would get me to a certain weight. The second time, I approached weight loss in a strength-based way. I figured out what was truly important to me. Then I re-joined the same weight-loss group, because there were things about the group that fit well with my newly defined goals. I needed the social support and accountability to keep me on track. I also liked the fact that I was able to talk about my journey with a group of people. What was new was that I was applying my strengths to my journey and finding my own way even as I worked within a weight-loss program.

This is the power of using your strengths. When I decided one of my do-able goals was to lose weight, I didn't have to re-invent the wheel. I simply joined a group I knew would work for me. I knew it would work because I had experience with it, which meant I could look at my past successes and build on them. I also knew it would work because it was a good fit with my strengths, since the choices of what to eat were left up to me. I'm a planner and critical thinker, so it's important to me to be able to plan things out my way, and there was a group of people I could share ideas with. I love to talk, but I'm also a good listener, and I learn things from other people's experiences. Last, I knew the group would work for me because it allowed me freedom to figure things out for myself rather than requiring I follow a pre-set diet. I'm good at following a pre-set diet, but I'm terrible at learning anything from it. In the long run, they don't work for me. My journey is ongoing. I'm living my plan every day and enjoying the journey.

Living Your Journey

Your journey is ongoing. It's important to love the journey you're on. Over time you may find you need to make adjustments to your short-term goals. You may find that something you've been doing that has worked for you stops working after a while. That's fine. Don't panic. Don't start thinking you've failed. All you need to do is revisit your do-able goals and make adjustments. Try a new approach, attitude, or way of thinking that lines up with your goals. Keep in mind that this journey is about change. It's about finding the best approach to making changes that are important to you. It isn't about holding yourself hostage to a rigid plan.

It's also possible that as you live out your journey, your long-term goal changes. That's fine. The nature of long-term goals is that they're *long-term*. They take time to achieve, and you're setting a goal based on what you know *right now*. The passing of time can change things in your life. Events happen that add depth and dimension to your goal. (If you need to understand how life can change long-term goals, go talk to any new mother.) Give yourself the grace to adjust your goal as you move along your map.

As you go through your day, you'll be able to keep your long-term goal in focus by looking at the steps you're taking right now (accomplishing short-term goals and taking small steps) in order to accomplish your larger goal.

In the following exercise you will keep track of your long- and short-term goals. This is an ongoing exercise that will be accomplished over days and weeks—for however long you feel it is helpful to you. There are two ways you can fill out the sheets. You can decide to fill them out once a day at the end of your day, or you can jot down different things at various times during the day. Either way, you'll be ensuring you're moving toward your goal as you keep track of your achievements throughout your day.

Begin by writing down your long-term goal—the large goal you're moving toward. Then write down any short-term goal or step you've taken that day that moves you toward your goal. Then answer the questions below in order to understand your journey better. By reflecting on things that made it easier for you to accomplish your short-term goal, you move closer to your long-term goal. Also, record which strengths you used to succeed, and then brainstorm other strengths you have that you can use to accomplish your short and long-term goals.

Use the example below to help you see what this exercise could look like filled out. It is taken from a woman whose goal is to find more joy and contentment in her life.

Living My Goal

Long-term goal: <u>To be at peace with myself, God, my family, and my life.</u>

Short-term goal: <u>I have two short-term goals today: Find something to be thankful for today. Do an act of kindness for someone else.</u>

Did I reach my short-term goal for today? <u>Yes.</u>

What things made it easier to reach my goal? <u>I prayed this morning before I went to work. I planned my act of kindness out and then did it when I had the chance.</u>

What strengths did I use to accomplish my goal? Spirituality and planning ahead.

What things made it hard to reach my goal? I was rushed for time, as usual, and I wasn't all that confident that my prayer was connecting with God. But when I was able to do my act of kindness, I figured God must have heard me. I felt wonderful afterward.

What other strengths do I have that can help? Love for myself and others. I'm finding I can reach out to others more than I thought I could. The acts of kindness are helping me see that I can connect with other people in a way that is healthy and makes me happy.

Now it's your turn:

Remember, there are no wrong answers. Spend a few minutes looking at what is going right and how you're meeting your short-term goals (and small steps) each day. You're walking step by step toward a new life.

Living My Goal

Long-term goal:

_____

_____

_____

_____

_____

Short-term goal:

_____

_____

_____

_____

_____

Did I reach my short-term goal for today?

_____

_____

_____

_____

What things made it easier to reach my goal?

_____

_____

_____

_____

What strengths did I use to accomplish my goal?

_____

_____

_____

_____

What things made it hard to reach my goal?

_____

_____

_____

_____

What other strengths do I have that can help?

_____

_____

_____

_____

_____

* * *

Long-term goal:

_____

_____

_____

_____

Short-term goal:

_____

_____

_____

_____

Did I reach my short-term goal for today?

_____

_____

_____

_____

What things made it easier to reach my goal?

_____

_____

_____

_____

_____

What strengths did I use to accomplish my goal?

_____

_____

_____

_____

_____

What things made it hard to reach my goal?

_____

_____

_____

_____

_____

What other strengths do I have that can help?

_____

_____

_____

_____

_____

* * *

Long-term goal:

_____

_____

_____

_____

Short-term goal:

_____

_____

_____

_____

_____

Did I reach my short term goal for today?

_____

_____

_____

_____

What things made it easier to reach my goal?

_____

_____

_____

_____

What strengths did I use to accomplish my goal?

_____

_____

_____

_____

What things made it hard to reach my goal?

_____

_____

_____

_____

_____

What other strengths do I have that can help?

_____

_____

_____

_____

_____

* * *

Long-term goal:

_____

_____

_____

_____

Short-term goal:

_____

_____

_____

_____

Did I reach my short term goal for today?

_____

_____

_____

What things made it easier to reach my goal?

_____

_____

_____

_____

What strengths did I use to accomplish my goal?

_____

_____

_____

_____

What things made it hard to reach my goal?

_____

_____

_____

_____

What other strengths do I have that can help?

_____

_____

_____

_____

Be kind to yourself while you're making changes. Change is always a process. Changing *behavior* is the goal, but it shouldn't be the thing you look at right away. Change begins inside you, in your mind, thoughts, attitudes, and emotions. Remember, too, that God is with you on your journey. He is helping you as you "change your mind" (see Romans 8:5-6). He's working for you and with you as you walk toward change. It's okay if you don't change everything overnight. It's not a sign of weakness or failure. It's a sign you're human. In the Bible, Paul talks about this very human process of change in Romans 7:7-21. The process of becoming all God intended us to be begins when we embrace everything that God has provided for us, starting with salvation through Jesus Christ and continuing with exploring and celebrating the amazing gifts He's given each of us. Salvation is about change, too. My husband is a pastor, and he tells me that about 33 different things happen to you at the moment you accept Christ as your personal Savior. That's a lot of change! God's nature is to give in abundance. He has provided for your every need. (See 2 Corinthians 9:8.)

In the next chapter you'll discover practical ways to be kind to yourself along the way.

Chapter 10

Kindness on the Journey

Rewards

Chapter 4 revealed that your habit or addiction was playing a role in your life—it served a purpose. It was something you wanted to change, but part of figuring out how to do it was to understand what need it was filling in your life.

We often use our addictions and habits as little rewards throughout the day. Think about a person who smokes cigarettes, for example. Have you ever heard a person who smokes say, "I've had a hard day; I'm going to go have a cigarette and relax"? Maybe you've had a time when you've looked at your addiction or habit and thought *Ahh—that's what I need—a little "me" time.* Or how about, *I've been so good lately, I deserve a little break.*

We often turn to our addictions and habits when we feel small, unhappy, disliked, tired, or depressed, because we believe they'll make us feel better. An important key to lifelong change is to use your strengths to find new, healthy ways to meet your needs and reward yourself.

It's okay to have needs. Sometimes we get caught up in the culture of Christianity that seems to tell us we should be perfect all the time, have it all figured out, be happy and self-sufficient. I'm all for being happy, but God created us with needs that we are required to meet. Look at Genesis 1:28-30. God created humanity for purposes, giving us responsibilities that fulfill our needs. In these three short verses we see that God gives us a need for companionship with God and each other (verse 28), to work and eat (verse 29), to share (verse 30——I love how God tells us to share His bounty with the beasts and the birds), and be good stewards of everything God has given us by taking care of it. You'll also find God-given needs in Genesis 2:15-25——a very good passage to spend time with while thinking about God's purpose for your life.

Having needs is not a sign of weakness; it's a sign of being human. The challenge comes when we go out looking for things to meet our needs. The world has lots to offer, but some of it actually ends up making things worse.

For example, when I was struggling with weight issues, I discovered I was using food to do things it can't do—was never intended to do. I was using food as a way to feel better (you may have heard the term "emotional eating"—that was me), to soothe my feelings of tiredness, social rejection, sadness, boredom—you name it. Of course, that strategy backfired on me, because as I continued to use food to do things it can't do, I got caught in a vicious cycle of overeating to feel better, so I then felt terrible because I was overweight and had no energy, so I'd eat to feel better—well, you can imagine where that got me.

Rewards That Work

Part of what I needed to do was to put food in its proper place in my life—sustenance. It's supposed to nourish my body, not be my best friend. But I also needed to find healthy ways to meet my emotional needs. They didn't go away when I changed my relationship with food. I used my strengths to find ways to meet those emotional needs in healthy ways. I love my husband very much, and I was able to bring him into my process by learning to share with him without expecting him to fix them or make them go away. For me, sharing my feelings with someone I trust is important, so I found ways to share my feelings with my husband rather than eat a corned beef sandwich. This had an added benefit; it strengthened our marriage. Now I use communication with my husband as a "reward" instead of chocolate bars.

Will what I did work for you? Maybe. Maybe not. The point isn't to duplicate what I do or anyone else does. It's to use your strengths to reward yourself throughout your day.

Another way to reward yourself could be to plan a larger reward at the end of a week or a month. This method helped me when I was beginning my weight-loss journey. I would reward myself once a week with a big ice cream sundae. Of course, I still rewarded myself in smaller ways each day, but having that big reward at the end of my week was something I looked forward to, which helped me make good food choices throughout the week.

A few years ago, I was hired by a non-profit agency to develop a strength-based program that would help women stop smoking. It was unprecedented in programming. There were no prototypes out there that I could look to for guidance. However, with prayer (lots of it), research, and time, I was able to develop an entire program. The time came to train individuals as to how to use this program.

Well into the training session, a trainee brought up an important issue about rewards. She was a tobacco specialist and had just returned from a tobacco control symposium where they had discussed the role of rewards in the stop-smoking process. The group of highly trained tobacco control specialists had been unable to come up with a satisfying answer to the question of rewards. They had tried to come up with a concrete "rewards" resource list. The list included the same old things as every other rewards list they had seen: "take a bubble bath," "go for a walk," or other such things. She told us that the problem was that the list was too general and was quickly dismissed by the individuals who were trying to overcome addiction. In short, while she believed learning to reward yourself in healthy ways was important, it was a concept that was difficult to "teach."

We decided to try to come up with a list of rewards of our own. It was difficult to think of things, and each time someone raised an idea, the tobacco specialist would give a weary smile and say, "Yeah, we thought of that." It turned out she was right—we couldn't come up with a good list of rewards that people should try.

The good you do today may be quickly forgotten, but the impact of what you do will never disappear (anonymous).

Then I asked the trainees to think about areas of their own lives they would like to see changed. Each person quickly identified an area he or she was currently working on. For one woman it was weight loss. Another person was struggling with an important relationship. Another was coping with a stressful situation at work.

I had them list their strengths. Then I asked them, "How can you reward yourself with what you love while staying committed to the change you want to make?"

Within moments people were coming up with rewards that would be meaningful to them. The person who was losing weight said, "Well, I love to cook. I love to make new recipes. But I want to lose weight, so . . ." She thought for a moment. "I can look at recipe books and get ideas for low-fat meals that my family will like." She went on to list several daily and weekly rewards that used her strengths. When she got finished, she was flushed with pleasure.

I loved the fact that she was able to see her love for cooking and food as a strength she could use to help herself lose weight. It would be tempting for someone in her position to think of a love of food as a "weakness" to overcome. She saw it for the fantastic strength it is.

Another trainee was working through a difficult relationship. She told us that she's a "people person," and that was one of the reasons this fractured relationship was so difficult for her to deal with. She often felt she needed a "boost" or "reward" to help her deal with the changes. She looked at her strength as a people person and quickly came up with a way to reward herself. She had a friend who was supportive of her that she knew she could call anytime day or night if she needed to, but she never had. She thought she should be able to plow through and deal with it alone. Not an easy task for a people person like her! She beamed as she told the group, "I can call a good friend and ask for some support or a kind word just to boost me up."

As you make your lifestyle change, it's important to think about ways to reward yourself throughout your day in new, healthy ways. These rewards are important to your journey, like finding beautiful flowers along the path; they serve as mood boosters and as a pat on the back for a job well done. Think about what would be an effective reward for you. It should be something that's quick, accessible, and that you're able to do several times a day. Think about the things you love to do, things that absorb you or that you look forward to doing. Work out ways to incorporate these healthy rewards into your daily routine. Making a change in your life is hard enough work, so be sure you reward yourself!

The example below will give you an idea of what this list of rewards could look like. Remember: use your strengths to decide what will work for you. It can also be helpful to review your responses to the questions in chapter 2 and chapter 3. Write down your strengths; then fill out the section called "My idea of a reward is . . ." and as many "How I'm going to do it" blanks as you can in one sitting. This can be completed in one sitting, taking 30 minutes or so. Other ideas may come to you later too. Jot them down as you think of them so that you have several choices of rewards that will work for you. Here's an example to help you on your way:

Rewards Example:

My Strengths: 1. <u>Humor</u>
2. <u>Daydreaming/planning</u>
3. <u>Creativity</u>
4. <u>Love of family and friends</u>

5. Critical thinking

My idea of a reward is—

- Listening to my favorite music—alone
- Picking up a new piece for my glass jar collection
- Chatting with a friend
- A date night with my spouse

How I'm going to do it—

- Jump into my car on my breaks and turn up the tunes
- Plan a shopping trip at the end of each month
- Call a friend on my lunch hour or after the kids are in bed
- Ask my spouse out on a date and *not* say where we're going. I'll have the whole thing planned out in advance

Now you try it:

Rewards

My Strengths: 1. _____
                  2. _____
                  3. _____
                  4. _____
                  5. _____

My idea of a reward is—

- _____
- _____
- _____
- _____

How I'm going to do it—

- _____
- _____
- _____
- _____

Including rewards in your change is an ongoing process. It happens over time, little by little. In the next chapter you'll find a chart that will help you celebrate your progress and your process.

In chapter 4, you looked closely at the thing you wanted to

change in order to understand it better. In chapter 12, you'll begin to examine the changes you've made in order to understand and appreciate them. You'll be keeping track of important moments of overcoming temptations, using strengths, rewarding yourself, and making gains.

Chapter 11

Taking Note of the Scenery

I'm sure you've discovered that the road to change is not a smooth, straight path. It's filled with bumps, curves, and the occasional rabbit trail. It can be challenging. In order to help you keep track of your successful changes, use the following "Strength to Change" Journal.

Like the "understanding journal" found in chapter 4, this is an ongoing journal—it's filled in over time. You'll fill out one row each day.

Choose a time of day to sit down and fill out a short journal of your day of successful change. Some people enjoy doing this in the evening, keeping it by their bedside and jotting down the events of the day before they go to sleep. Others prefer the morning, reflecting on the previous day. Each entry will take less than 30 minutes.

Each day you'll reflect on your feelings about your changing life, make note of at least one positive change you made and how you used your strengths to accomplish it. You'll also note at least one way you rewarded yourself that day and how it worked for you. Next you'll write how you're feeling *at that moment* about your accomplishments, and you'll think about some of the gains you've made in your life. Finally, you'll jot down a prayer, word of thanks, or petition to God as you finish reflecting on your day.

Keep your journals over time, and every once in a while go back and read old entries. You'll be thrilled and will praise God to see how far you've come.

I've included an example for you to look at so you can better understand what the chart could look like filled out. The example is taken from someone who is on a journey toward becoming a smoke-free person.

"Strength to Change" Journal

I'm changing my life today!	☺ Feeling good!
Positive changes I made today:	Went out with friend who smokes. But I didn't smoke with her!
How I used my strengths to do it:	I thought about my young daughter and how much I love her and how I want to be a good example to her. So I used my strength of love for my family and stayed in the restaurant when my friend went outside to smoke!
Ways I rewarded myself today:	I found a big jar, and I'm filling it with the money I would have spent on cigarettes. Just looking at the jar full of money makes me happy.
How I used my strengths to do it:	I have the strength of planning and organizing. I've used that strength to make plans for the money in the jar. We're planning a camping trip this summer—something we couldn't afford before!
How I feel about my accomplishments:	Good. Kind of proud of myself, actually.
Gains I have made in my life:	I've gone five days as a non-smoker. I actually feel better. I'm coughing a lot, but I know that's helping my lungs to clear. I love to picture my lungs turning a healthy pink.
Gains I have made in my plans for the future:	I'm making a safe home for my family and myself by sparing them from secondhand smoke. And my daughter says she isn't as worried about my health as she was before.

Prayer:	Thank you, God, for my family and how they support this change. I'm excited as I become a smoke-free person. I know there will be times when I want to smoke, and I pray that you'll be right there with me, helping me to resist.

"Strength to Change" Journal
Recording my healthy lifestyle

I'm changing my life today!

Positive changes I made today:

How I used my strengths to do it:

Ways I rewarded myself today:

How I used my strengths to do it:

How I feel about my accomplishments:

Gains I have made in my life:

Gains I have made in my plans for the future:

Prayer:

"Strength to Change" Journal
Recording my healthy lifestyle

I'm changing my life today!

Positive changes I made today:

How I used my strengths to do it:

Ways I rewarded myself today:

How I used my strengths to do it:

How I feel about my accomplishments:

Gains I have made in my life:

Gains I have made in my plans for the future:

Prayer:

Remember to fill in the chart each day. If you miss a day, just pick it up the next day and record the day you're on.

In the next chapter you'll discover how other people can help you make the change that's important to you.

We are not power-less specks of dust drift-ing around in the wind. We are, each of us, like beautiful snowflakes, unique and born for a specific reason and purpose (Elisabeth Kübler-Ross).

Chapter 12

Social Support

Rallying the Troops! Getting Support for Your Changing Lifestyle

Change means disruption. You well know that by now. The effort you're putting into your lifestyle change is tremendous, and you want it to last a lifetime. By using your strengths to change your life, you're ensuring the easiest, most authentic change possible. However, disruption in your life causes disruption for others as well. You may find there are people who seem less than thrilled with the changes you've made in your life, while others cheer you on (or maybe even join you!). It's important to have people on your side—cheering for you, supporting you, offering you an ear when you need it. It's how God created you. Genesis 2:18 tells us that God created us to be in community with one another—-that it's "not good" to be alone.

You need a suitable helper, too. Who is your suitable helper? The answer will depend a great deal on your context (where you live, who lives with you, if you work outside the home, if you have a church you regularly attend, and other things like that), and it's possible you aren't certain who your best helper (supporter) is. That's what you're about to take a look at.

Let's start at the top: God. People of faith understand that God is as close as "right here." We believe that we communicate with God through prayer, reading the Bible, and being in community with other Christians. There's a strong understanding that God is present in the lives of His people.

I was speaking with a man who was going through a difficult time. At the end of our conversation, I asked if I could pray with him, and his response was, "Yes, pray that God will show up in the midst of my circumstances."

Are you waiting for God to show up in the midst of your change? The good news is He's not going to "show up"—He's already here, with you, right now, where you are. Romans 8:15-16, 35-39 tells us that our relationship with God is a "family" relationship. We've been given the gift of the Holy Spirit, and nothing can cause "Abba," our Heavenly Daddy, to abandon us.

Laughter is the closest distance between two people (Victor Borge).

You could put this book down right now and whisper to Him, and He would hear you. He's there beside you and has been the whole time.

Take a moment right now to ask God to help you see the many ways He's been at work in your life over the past year. Psalm 46:1 tells us that God is "ever present" with us. Most often we see God's presence in our lives indirectly. Think of it like throwing a stone into a still pond. The stone hits the water and creates ripples on it. The stone itself is out of sight, but you can continue to see the effect it has on the water long after it drops from view.

Whenever I stop to reflect on what God has been doing in my life, I'm always struck by two things: First, that He is so very involved in the details of my life, working out things I can't see or even know about. Second, I'm always overcome with gratitude and praise. For me, there is a profound sense of privilege that God is with me, looking out, caring for me and my family. I know He's also present and active in your life.

Not feeling like God is right there with you? That's okay. You can take a few minutes right now to take a look at how to begin to see and understand the closeness of God in ways He knows are meaningful to you. God's presence in your life, as His child, is truth. It's important to know that when we go looking for God in our lives, we'll find Him. (See Proverbs 8:17; Jeremiah 29:13; Luke 11:10.)

You can finish this exercise in one sitting in about an hour. When you have completed it, spend the rest of the day thinking about your answers. Add any new thoughts you have to your original answers.

Begin by answering the questions below (be as open and honest as you can.) Sometimes we get caught up on what we believe the "right" answers are. That's fine, but what's really important is that you answer the questions based on your experience, thoughts, and desires. I've filled in an example for you. Use it only as a guide to show you what it might look like to answer these questions. I've given you answers that are general to many people's experiences and expectations but may not be to yours.

1. **In what ways do you expect God to communicate with you?** God speaks through the Bible—sometimes I can recall a verse I've read before at a time when I need it. Sometimes when I pray, I feel a "calm assurance," a feeling of peace. Sometimes I think about a situation and can sense God saying, *It's going to be okay.* God can and has spoken to people in an audible voice.

2. **In what ways do you expect God to reveal to you His presence in your life?** When I think back on certain times or events in my life, I can see how God did things that were beyond my ability to do. God sends other people into my life to encourage me and pray for and with me. God gives me opportunities to help and serve others. He has answered prayer. Others have told me they see God doing something in my life. I have had times when I felt God was close to me.

3. **How would you know if God was present with you right now?** I could pray, believing He hears me. I could choose to believe the promises I find in Scripture. I can spend quiet time listening, be-

lieving God will speak to me in a way I understand. I might feel His presence with me or within me.

Now it's your turn. Spend time thinking and reflecting on your past and present relationship with God. Begin by answering the following questions. Be as open and honest as you can. Sometimes we get caught up on what we believe the "right" answers are. That's fine, but what's really important is that you answer the questions based on your experience, thoughts, and desires:

1. In what ways do you expect God to communicate with you?

_____

_____

_____

_____

2. In what ways do you expect God to reveal to you His presence in your life?

_____

_____

_____

_____

3. How would you know if God was present with you right now?

_____

_____

_____

_____

As I worked through the questions above for myself, I couldn't help but feel wonderful about the many ways God has spoken to me and made His presence known to me in the past and present. The longer I thought about these precious (and sometimes difficult) times, the more excited I became, knowing God really is with me.

Now it's time to build on the reflections you've just experienced. Think about the past year and the different ways you've been able to see and identify God working in your life. Answer the following questions as fully and honestly as you can. I've given you examples filled in with general thoughts, ideas, and experiences that could be typical but may not reflect your own experience.

1. **How I've seen God working in my life in the past year:** I've seen God working in my son's life by helping him change his attitude toward other people. I've seen God provide money to me when I needed it most. I've seen how God has directed me to my new job, even though I wasn't sure I should take it. I've seen how God has led me to become more active in my church. I see how God has helped me find friends in our new neighborhood. I've seen God answer prayer. I've seen new doors open to me.

2. **How I've seen God working in my life in the past three months:** God has led me to a place where I can see things that I need to change in my life. I've seen Him working in other people's lives and heard testimonies of how He has changed them.

3. **How I've seen God working in my life this week:** As I've worked through this book, I see more clearly how God is active in my life. I've been able to make changes that just a few weeks ago I didn't think I could make. I feel better. I've begun to see that God loves me and isn't going to hurt my feelings or bully me as I change, but that He wants to help me because He loves me.

4. **How I've seen God working in my life today:** I found I wanted to pray today, which is new for me. I was able to deal with a temptation today. I overcame a craving. I looked up some of the Scripture verses given in this book and found I wanted to read more.

Now it's your turn to reflect on how God has been at work in your life over time. This is a joyful and life-affirming exercise that will bring you peace. Take your time as you think about the last year, but try to finish the exercise in one sitting if possible.

1. **How I've seen God working in my life in the past year:**

_____

_____

_____

_____

_____

2. **How I've seen God working in my life in the past three months:**

_____

_____

_____

_____

_____

3. **How I've seen God working in my life this week:**

_____

_____

_____

_____

_____

4. **How I've seen God working in my life today:**

_____

_____

_____

_____

_____

One of the great things about God is that He loves to give good gifts to His children. Read Matthew 7:11. Here Jesus tells us that our Heavenly Father wants to give us the things we need to live happy lives.

One of those good gifts to each of us is the gift of family and friends. You may have people already cheering for you, and that's fantastic. If not, you can begin to reach out to others for their support.

The changes you're making in your life affect the people around you. It's important that you have friends and family members around you who support your decision to make a change.

It would be great if everyone you knew and spent time with supported you all the way, but that may not be the case. Sometimes the changes you make cause someone else to feel uncomfortable, and he or she may react to that discomfort by seeming to be unsupportive. The truth is that you don't need everyone you know to support your changes. You do need a few people close to you whom you can count on. As long as you have one or two truly supportive people, you're doing fine.

It's important to be wise about whom to approach for support. In general, most of us need support from the people who are closest to us. If you're married, for example, it would be important to know your spouse was cheering for you and supporting you as you make a change. For most of us, one close friend whom we trust is also very helpful.

I think it's a mistake to think that everyone should support us as we change. I like to share my dreams and hopes with those who are closest to me and know me well. For me, this is usually just my husband, but I have two close friends I know I can talk to about anything.

It's sometimes difficult to ask for support. To help you work through this, I've included an exercise to help you clarify for yourself who you really need support from, what that person(s) can say and do to be supportive (for example, what "support" means to you), and the things about making a change that you find the most difficult. From there you can build a strategy for getting support that is meaningful to you from the people you need support from the most.

This is a quick exercise you can do in just a few minutes. I've included an example of what it might look like to fill out these questions. These are general examples and may not reflect your experience.

Getting the Support I Need

Write a list of the people whom you need support from the most:

My spouse

My friend Judy

My father

Write about one person who already supports your decision to change. What does that person *do* to encourage you? What does that person *say* to encourage you? My husband tells me he sees a change already and that he's proud of me. My friend treated me to a girls' night out, and we went to dinner and a movie, just us girls. She said she did it because she sees how hard I'm working to make this change and how well I'm doing.

Write about the things that you would like to tell this person about the changes you're making in your life. Use "I" statements. "I sometimes struggle with the changes I'm making, and I'd like to be able to call you during those times when I feel like giving up." Or "I like it when you tell me I'm a good person. I need that encouragement."

Write about the positive changes you've made and how they are impacting your life. Share these accomplishments with someone who supports your efforts to change. I've made changes in my house that reflect my new lifestyle. I've started to take better care of myself. I've found a deeper connection with God. I've learned so much about myself and can see so many positive things I couldn't see before. I'm more positive in my attitude toward other things as well. I see hope, and I believe I can change.

Look back at your list of people whose support you would like most right now. How can you ask for support? What things could you ask of each of these people that would help him or her support you? <u>I would like my father and my husband to sometimes ask me how I'm doing. I like it when they do this, as it shows me they're thinking of me. I would like my father to tell me he's proud of me. I would like to be able to share my feelings with my husband.</u>

Use the statements above to open up a conversation with the person who is supportive of the changes you're making. Talking with someone you trust about the things that are important to you helps both of you. It helps you by talking out your ideas, hopes, and feelings, and it helps the relationship between the two of you stay strong and healthy.

I will talk to <u>My father</u>
When: <u>tonight, after dinner</u>

Fill out the exercise below to help you understand the support you already have and any additional support you need and from whom. Try to do the exercise in one sitting. When deciding whom to talk to and when, choose a time in the not-too-distant future. For example, if you decide you want to speak to a friend and ask for support, choose a time that same day or the next day to speak to him or her. If you choose a time too far off in the future, it will be difficult to keep that date.

Write a list of the people whom you need support from the most:

_____

_____

_____

_____

_____

Write about one person who already supports your decision to change. What does that person *do* to encourage you? What does that person *say* to encourage you?

_____

_____

_____

_____

_____

Write about the things that you would like to tell this person about the changes you're making in your life. Use "I" statements.

_____

_____

_____

_____

_____

Write about the positive changes you've made and how they are impacting your life. Share these accomplishments with someone who supports your efforts to change.

_____

_____

_____

_____

Look back at your list of people whose support you would like most right now. How can you ask for support? What things could you ask of each of these people that would help him or her support you?

_____

_____

_____

_____

Use the statements above to open up a conversation with the person who is supportive of the changes you're making. Talking with someone you trust about the things that are important to you helps both of you. It helps you by talking out your ideas, hopes, and feelings, and it helps the relationship between the two of you stay strong and healthy.

I will talk to _____

When: _____

Support while we change is important. Understanding what kind of support we need helps us to understand ourselves and what we can reasonably expect from the people in our lives.

The support you have from God goes far beyond anything we can experience from anyone else. God is with you in very real, sometimes tangible ways. Also, keep in mind, too, that God is the one who has brought these wonderful, supportive people into your life.

Chapter 13

Walking Toward Success

You have a lot to celebrate in your life right now. You've taken many steps in your journey toward a new, healthier, happier future. You've begun to gain momentum in your process of change. You're no longer drawing your map—you're following it, trekking across the landscape with confidence. Take a moment to reflect on your success. Write about the joy you've experienced, the successes you've accomplished, and the people who have helped you make this important change. Then take time to offer to God a prayer of thanksgiving, praise, and acknowledgement for who He is and what He is accomplishing in your life.

1. What are you enjoying the most about the changes you've made in your life?

_____

_____

_____

_____

_____

2. What things are you able to do now that you weren't able to do, or not able to do as easily before you made this change in your life?

_____

_____

_____

_____

_____

3. Write about one person who supports your changes. What does that person do to encourage you? What does that person say to encourage you?

_____

_____

_____

_____

_____

4. My prayer of thanksgiving, praise, and acknowledgement to God for the things He has done:

_____

_____

_____

_____

_____

_____

Hills to Climb on the Journey

Using your strengths to change your life makes the journey easier. That isn't to say there aren't challenges. As you walk the map you've created, you may be finding some sections are like driving on a highway on a clear day—smooth sailing. Other times, the journey might feel more like a hike through the forest—interesting, but slow going, putting one foot in front of the other. Other times, the journey feels like climbing a rocky cliff—hanging on for dear life.

For many of us, those rocky climbs have a great deal to do with our feelings—our emotions. Sometimes strong emotions can cloud the path and get in the way of your goal. Even though emotions are temporary—they change over time depending on circumstances, time of day, health, stress, and even diet— they deserve taking the time to recognize them and work with them. We are told in 2 Corinthians 10:5 that God has given us the ability, through Him, to control our thoughts and emotions in order to live vic- torious lives in Christ. If you've had times in the past when you've felt sad, tired, angry, or over- whelmed, chances are good that you'll experience those feelings as you walk through your changes. If your feelings go unchecked, they can sometimes have the power to derail the efforts you're making to change your life. In this chapter you'll learn how to apply your strengths to the emotional part of the journey.

Joy is a prayer—Joy is strength—Joy is love—Joy is a net of love by which you can catch souls (Mother Teresa of Calcutta).

Feelings aren't weaknesses; they're normal. However, there can be times when your feelings may be very strong and might lead you to a place where you're in danger of losing some of the important gains you've made. When this happens, it's important to know how to manage your feelings. Managing your feelings means that you apply your strengths to the times when your feelings are so strong that you feel you're no longer in control of them—they could lead you into returning to your old ways, habits, or addictions.

There are steps you can take to help you control your emotions so they don't control you. This exercise is ongoing and can be done in two or more sittings. Complete the first section in one sitting, and fill in your strengths. If you can, go on to complete the third section of the exercise. If you need to, you can complete the third section later in the day, or no later than the following day.

First, you need to acknowledge your feelings. This usually means taking a moment to look honestly at what you're feeling. It may sound simple, but when feelings are running high, it can take practice. For example, I have moments when I look at my two wonderful kids and just think: *Go play somewhere else! Just leave me alone for a while.* When I take a step back and look at my true feelings I usually find one of two things. Either I'm tired, or I'm hungry. I'm usually not angry, upset, or even frustrated. When I figured this out, it helped me change my reaction to my children when I felt they were getting on my nerves. Life is calmer for me now, not because my children stopped being loud and playing noisy games, but because I understand where my feelings are coming from, and I can take steps to solve the problem without blowing up at my kids.

After you've spent time thinking about what you're feeling and when, remind yourself of your strengths by writing them out. Then you'll link the feelings and the strengths together in order to form a strategy for how to manage your feelings when you need to.

Follow the example below, which will help you see what this exercise could look like filled out. Remember to take time to honestly consider your feelings and emotions. Feel them, experience them, and then identify the source when you can. This will take time and practice. Some of the feelings will relate more to walking away from addictions, as to cigarettes, drugs, or alcohol. Others will relate to more habitual changes, or lifestyle changes. There is also space for you to write down your own emotions and feelings that are not expressed in the list.

The example reflects the journey of a person who is moving toward higher self-esteem and self-love. It is a reflection of the feelings she has had over a period of a week, relating to the changes she is making in her life.

<u>X</u>   **I feel as if something is missing somehow.**
      When? <u>When I'm in a crowd. I'm used to hanging back,</u>
           <u>feeling sorry for myself. That part is gone, and it's</u>
           <u>weird sometimes.</u>

___   I feel angry.
        When? _____
        _____
        _____
        _____
        _____

___   I feel sad.
        When? _____
        _____
        _____
        _____
        _____

_X_   I feel as if I'm tired of trying.
        When? <u>When my boyfriend and I have a fight. I feel as if I</u>
              <u>just want to run back to my old ways of comforting</u>
              <u>myself.</u>

___   I feel like taking a break from changing.
        When? _____
        _____
        _____
        _____
        _____

_X_   I feel confused about what I'm doing.
        When? <u>When I get advice from my parents and siblings *and*</u>
              <u>friends all at once. I feel as if I don't even know what</u>
              <u>I'm doing.</u>

___   I feel restless.
        When? _____
        _____
        _____
        _____
        _____

___ **I feel fine; then I'm suddenly angry.**
When? _____
_____
_____
_____
_____

___ **I feel frustrated.**
When? _____
_____
_____
_____
_____

_X_ **Other feelings I've had:** <u>I've been feeling nervous some-</u>
<u>times.</u>
When? <u>When I think about my future, I sometimes feel ner-</u>
<u>vous, because I'm not sure what to expect anymore.</u>

Check off the feelings you've experienced, or write in feelings
and emotions you've had since you began your journey of change.
Then jot down when you've experienced them.

___ **I feel as if something is missing somehow.**
When? _____
_____
_____
_____
_____

___ **I feel angry.**
When? _____
_____
_____
_____

___ **I feel sad, as if I'm missing a friend.**
When? _____
_____

_____

_____

_____

__ I feel that I can overcome the craving.

When? _____

_____

_____

_____

_____

__ I feel like taking a break from changing.

When? _____

_____

_____

_____

_____

__ I don't seem to be fighting with cravings.

When? _____

_____

_____

_____

_____

__ I feel restless.

When? _____

_____

_____

_____

_____

__ I feel fine; then I'm suddenly angry.

When? _____

_____

_____

_____

_____

___ I feel frustrated.
      When? _____

            _____
            _____
            _____
            _____

___ Other feelings I've had: _____
      When? _____

            _____
            _____
            _____
            _____

Now that you've had a good hard look at your feelings, it's time to apply your strengths to the situation. First remind yourself of your strengths. You might list the same strengths you've always listed, or you may add to the list some strengths that you've rediscovered over the course of your journey.

My Strengths: 1. Spirituality
                2. Communication
                3. Organization/keeping a clean house
                4. Love for the outdoors
                5. Energy/enthusiasm

My Strengths: 1. _____
                2. _____
                3. _____
                4. _____
                5. _____

Next you'll combine your feelings with your strengths in order to brainstorm ways that you can gain control over your feelings. Remember: feelings are normal, and you're not trying to stop yourself from having difficult feelings and emotions. You're only working to control them so they don't have control over you.

Follow this example:

Thinking Through My Feelings

The Feeling	The Strength I Can Use	How I Will Do It
As if something is missing somehow	Energy/enthusiasm	I'll give myself a pep talk before a gathering and remind myself of all the great things I have to offer to the event.
Tired of trying	Love for outdoors	When I argue with my boyfriend, I can take a break and clear my head with a walk or a ride on my bike.
Confused about what I'm doing	Communication	I can write my family a letter, letting each of them know I love them and saying exactly what kind of support I need from them.
Nervous about the future	Spirituality	I can pray and read my Bible. I can also ask others to pray for me as I slowly learn to trust God more and more about the future.

Now it's your turn.

Thinking Through My Feelings

The Feeling	The Strength I Can Use	How I Will Do It

Chapter 14

Reflecting on the Map

You've accomplished amazing things in the time you've been on this journey toward change. Let's reflect on what steps you've taken and the gains you've made.

- You've gained control over your situation; it no longer has control over you.

- You've refocused your life from one that was threatening to center around a problem to a life that centers on God, the things He has provided for you, and His profound love for you.

- You've answered the question of your personal *how?*—how you work, how you think, how to find out what is important to you.

- You've discovered that your identity is found in God, the One who created you, gifted you, and has been with you from the very beginning. You've deepened your connection to God, the One who knows you better than you know yourself.

- You've examined your strengths, the things you love, the things you're good at, the things that absorb you. You explored them, celebrated them, and thanked God for them.

- You faced your addiction and cut it down to size by realizing it wasn't as overwhelming as you had once thought. You took control of your hot spots.
- You've offered your strengths back to God, who showed you a depth and richness about them that only He could show you.
- You began to draw your map by finding the "You Are Here" spot. To do this, you daydreamed about the future you want and the things you are looking forward to.
- You weighed out your true thoughts and feelings about making some kind of a change in your life right now.
- Your next step was to break down your large goal into bite-size "do-able" pieces. You discovered what things were truly important to you.
- You reflected on your past in terms of what you did right and how you could build on those successes. This was an act of self-love and an act of worship.
- You jumped into the change room of your life to try on new behaviors and new ways of thinking. You used your strengths to help guide choices as to which new behaviors and ways of thinking could work for you. You looked into the mirror of prayer, using God's view of you as your guide. You discovered how in God's eyes you are lovely, loveable, and filled with purpose.
- You reflected on your experience, trying on new ways of thinking and doing, and wrote about what you accomplished, the strengths you used, and how they helped you decide about the goal. You also offered each goal up to God in prayer.
- You pulled patterns from your experiences, trying on new ways of thinking and doing, and you discovered your true long-term goal. You astonished yourself when you wrote down the gains you've made in your physical and mental health, home life, self-confidence, plans for the future, and relationship with God. This showed you how far you had already come in your journey.

- From there, you filled in the road to your long-term goal with short-term goals, doable strategies that would move you daily toward your goal. You examined which strengths you used to accomplish your goals, and you thought about additional strengths you have that could also help you reach your destination.

  The first step to getting the things you want out of life is this: Decide what you want (Ben Stein).

- You learned about the importance of being kind to yourself every day and rewarding your efforts as you blaze the trail toward change. You discovered how to use your strengths to determine what kind of rewards are meaningful to you and how you can meet your needs in healthy ways.

- Next, you kept a journal highlighting the positive changes you've made in your life, the strengths you've used to accomplish them, and the prayers you've offered of thanksgiving, praise, and petition to God.

- You've built a support network that includes God, family, friends, church, or other important people who support the positive changes in your life.

- Then you reflected on the things you enjoy the most about the changes you've made in your life.

- You've created a system, using your strengths, that helps you take control of your feelings and emotions when they threaten to overwhelm you.

You've lived your map. You've walked your journey. Celebrate your accomplishments by acknowledging the gains you've made in every area of your life.

Gains Example

Write down some of the important gains you've made in your life so far on this journey:

1. Gains I have made in my physical and mental health:

_____

_____

_____

_____

2. Gains I have made in my home life:

_____

_____

_____

3. Gains I have made in my self-confidence:

_____

_____

_____

4. Gains I have made in my plans for the future:

_____

_____

_____

5. Gains I have made in my relationship with God:

_____

_____

_____

Laying it to Rest: Rituals of Change

You've gained control over an important part of your life. It no longer has control of you. It's important to celebrate that change in a way that lays the issue to rest. It's time to seal closed the door to the past.

It's helpful to mark transitions in our life by a ritual. We do this all the time. For example, when a couple gets married, it's traditional to have a ceremony that makes it official. When a person graduates from high school, there's a graduation ceremony, and a diploma is presented. We make a big deal out of these things for a good reason: They *are* a big deal.

You've accomplished so much. It's important to mark the occasion in some way. How you choose to mark the moment depends on how you're feeling about your accomplishment. If you're feeling over-the-top happy, then a party may be a good marker for you. If you're feeling more as though you've just won the battle of your life, then it may be meaningful to you to "bury the enemy"—perhaps take a shoebox with an object that symbolizes what you've overcome and bury it in the backyard. It might be helpful to create a physical marker such as stones piled up in a section of your yard or a homemade stepping stone with the date you made the change in your life. You could record the date in your journal or Bible so you can refer back to it over time.

Use your strengths to help you decide the best way to mark your moment. Complete the promises below to remind you of how important it is to mark it. Use it to start planning this important occasion.

How I will mark my moment:

_____

_____

_____

_____

_____

When I will mark my moment:

_____

_____

_____

_____

Who will be there with me to mark my moment:

_____

_____

_____

_____

Chapter 15
Maintaining the Change

You're no longer bound by the things that once held you down. You're free from the things that tried to keep you in bondage.

The closer you get to God, the farther away you move from those things that would steal your joy, your hope, your love, your sense of freedom, and your purpose in life. Your ever-closer relationship with the living God is leading you toward living life to the fullest.

It's not that problems won't come. They will. It's a fact of being on the earth, living and breathing the air. But you're able to face the problems of life in a new, healthy, confident way. You understand how amazing you are because that's what God created you to be. You're able to prevent certain problems from occurring in your life, because you can now recognize when they're coming and cut them off long before they reach you.

A life lived connected to your strengths—connected to the Giver of strengths—is a life unfettered and unhindered by the drudgery of harmful habits, deadly addictions, secret sins, and painful pasts.

You've shown tremendous grace and courage in these past weeks as you've drawn your map and walked the path you created using your strengths. The journey you've mapped out is just the beginning of a new life. The future that is set out before you is one that is limitless in the hope it holds.

Finding your strengths is the gateway to the adventure of your life (Bonnie Grove).

This is really exciting! There's no turning back from here. It's full steam ahead with God from here.

The exercises in this chapter will help you solidify your goals and your ability to meet your goals both now and in the future. Do these quickly, answering with the first response that comes to your mind. This is the truest indication of where you are in your journey. It will take less than 30 minutes.

Remember to be reflective and honest with your responses. It is far more beneficial for you to know where you are than it is for you to worry about where you think you should be. Let's begin by looking at how you're thinking and feeling about your journey today:

What is your goal now about your habit, addiction, or old way of behaving or thinking?

    a. Go back to the way things were

    b. Control where and when I engage in my old habit, addiction, or ways of behaving or thinking

    c. Not sure of my goal

    d. Remain on the road toward change

How likely do you think it is that you'll return to your habit, addiction, or old way of behaving or thinking?

    a. Extremely or somewhat likely

    b. Not very likely

    c. Not at all likely

As your journey in life continues, you'll need to remind yourself occasionally what it is you really want and what you are doing to ensure you get it.

Life is busy, but you can stay focused on your goal as you live your life because of how well you now understand yourself and how you work. You know what you want, and you know effective ways to accomplish what you want.

Thinking of the present and the future, fill in the chart below in order to stay on the path you've forged in your life. The example is taken from a person who has walked away from an addiction. Use this chart as an ongoing encouragement for your new lifestyle. I recommend keeping it in a place where you'll see it often, adding to it whenever you've tried something new that has worked for you.

Follow this example:

Maintaining My Strengths-filled Life

This is what I know I want	This is what I am doing to ensure I get what I want
To remain a smoke-free person for the rest of my life!	I've made my house smoke-free, and no one is allowed to smoke in it.
	I let visiting family and friends know ahead of time that I am a non-smoker and that they are welcome to smoke outside only. I also make sure I don't go with them outside while they smoke.
	I'm remembering to reward myself in small ways every day and in larger ways every month.

Now it's your turn:

Maintaining My Strengths-filled Life

This is what I know I want	This is what I am doing to ensure I get what I want

What's It All For?

You've been on an amazing journey, but life keeps going! And so will your journey. Having successfully made a positive change in your life is fantastic. Using your strengths to change your life has placed you on the map of your life, and there's no turning back. God has filled you with great gifts, talents, and strengths for a purpose that goes even beyond making a lifestyle change. He wants to take you deeper into the adventure of your life.

Yes, God wants you to be happy, but the purpose of finding and using your strengths goes far beyond just living a happy life. It is about finding your true identity in Christ and living fully in the power of God daily. When you know what your strengths are, you're better able to see and understand your connection to God. Connecting to God leads you into a deeper relationship with Him. You've discovered this already as you've worked with God to discover the amazing gifts He has given you and how they work.

Reaching Out to Others

One of the best ways to stay on your path is to reach out to someone else who is looking to make a change in his or her life. Sharing your story with someone can have a huge impact on that person's life. Offer encouragement and non-judgmental support to this person. You'll help him or her, and it will help you stay on the path you want to be on.

What's great about the strength-based approach is that the pressure is off you. You don't need to be an "expert" about anything in order to reach out to someone. You just need to share your story, listen to that person, and help the person find his or her strengths. Your friend can draw his or her map, just as you did, when he or she is supported and honestly cared about. There's simply no greater thing we can do for each other than to love each other. Read John 13:14-17, 34-35. Here Jesus tells His friends that they will be identified in the world as being followers of Him because of the love they show toward each other.

In chapter 1 we explored some ideas around empowerment and how it's about each person finding the desire and the ability to rise up and look for solutions to problems. You're in a place of empowerment today because of the time and effort you've put into self-reflection, prayer, planning, and understanding yourself.

You're able to seek out solutions to issues in your life based on what you know is going to work for you. That is an exciting place to be in.

You can help other people get there, too. You won't need to go tell other people what things they should change or even that they need to change. Just share your story with anyone who cares to listen. When someone asks you to help him or her make a change in his or her life, you can help that person find his or her strengths, then work through the same process you did.

Walk in gentleness and love, and the love of Christ will change your world.

When Love Hurts provides practical and scriptural tools to help you reclaim your sense of well-being and change the dysfunctional course of your relationships.

When Love Hurts
10 Principles to Transform Difficult Relationships
By Karla Downing
ISBN-13: 978-0-8341-2136-2

BEACON HILL PRESS
OF KANSAS CITY

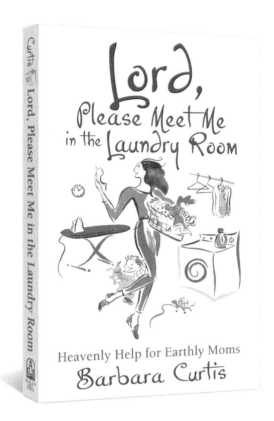
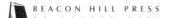

Bridge the gap to better connections.

Through encouragement and introspection, this practical book helps you connect your spiritual life and your daily interactions with the people you love as God begins to change you from the inside out.

A WOMAN and HER

Relationships

Transforming the Way We Connect

Rosemary Flaaten

A Woman and Her Relationships
Transforming the Way We Connect
Rosemary Flaaten
ISBN: 978-0-8341-2338-0
Available wherever books are sold

BEACON HILL PRESS
OF KANSAS CITY

DO YOU HAVE TOO MUCH STUFF?

Learn to de-clutter your heart and home with this practical and insightful book from Beacon Hill Press.

Too Much Stuff
De-Cluttering Your Heart and Home
By Kathryn Porter
ISBN-13: 978-0-8341-2256-7

BEACON HILL PRESS
OF KANSAS CITY